The 25 Days of
Christmas

*Family Readings, Scriptures, and Activities
for the Advent Season*

GREG JOHNSON

W PUBLISHING GROUP
A Division of Thomas Nelson Publishers
Since 1798

www.wpublishinggroup.com

THE 25 DAYS OF CHRISTMAS
Greg Johnson

© 2004 by Greg Johnson. Published by W Publishing Group, a Division of Thomas Nelson, Inc., P.O. Box 141000, Nashville, Tennessee 37214.

All Scripture quotations, unless otherwise indicated, are taken from The New Century Version ®. Copyright © 1987, 1988, 1991 by Thomas Nelson, Inc. All rights reserved.

Quotations designated NIV are from The Holy Bible, New International Version. Copyright © 1973, 1978, 1984, International Bible Society. Used by permission of Zondervan Bible Publishers.

Quotations designated NLT are from the Holy Bible, New Living Translation (Wheaton, Ill.: Tyndale House Publishers, 1996). Used by permission.

Library of Congress Cataloging-in-Publication Data

Johnson, Greg, 1956–
    The 25 days of Christmas : family readings and Scriptures for the Advent season / by Greg Johnson.
        p. cm.
        ISBN 0-8499-1835-9 (hardcover)
    1. Advent—Prayer books and devotions—English.   2. Christmas—Prayer-books and devotions—English.   3. Family—Prayer-books and devotions—English.   I. Title.
BV40.J64   2004
249—dc22   2004010081

Printed in the United States of America
04 05 06 07 08   QW   5 4 3 2

Contents

Introduction

Making Christmas meaningful . . . or not making Christmas meaningful? Having the family pause every day for quiet reflection on Jesus Christ and God's plan for man . . . or allowing this Christmas to be like every other, emphasizing decorations and gifts, but not much pause on the reason for the season?

Good questions, but I never seem to get to the obvious answer I always want. It takes me two days to get my Christmas lights up on the house (okay, I go overboard), another day to decorate the tree and the rest of the home (which includes about seventy porcelain houses I arrange into three different "villages"), two or more Christmas parties, work, buying presents . . . sheesh!

No wonder I usually wait until Christmas Eve service to ponder the true meaning of this high and holy season.

If you're looking for something that the family can gather around a few minutes a day during December, these pages should relieve some of the guilt—and pressure—to make this Christmastime more meaningful than years past.

I paged through and read more than one hundred books on Christmas and Jesus. I discovered four main topics are discussed:

- Jesus,
- Mary and Joseph (and angels),
- the wise men, shepherds, and Herod, and
- the importance of family and making each Christmas better than the previous.

This book will follow the same outline, but with some significant variety to it.

Not many of us have the time to spend thirty minutes, either alone or with our families, to prepare ourselves *every day* for making Christmas fuller and more special than any Christmas before. This book gives you five-, ten-, and twenty-minute options.

Introduction

Five Minutes: If you just want to read Scripture each day, this book has a daily guide.

Ten Minutes: If you want Scripture and a story or meditation, this book has it.

Twenty-Minutes: If you want Scripture, a story or meditation, and some other features, this book also has . . .

- tips on Christmas and ideas of how to make the season even better,
- Christmas carols,
- short "Family Moments" where you can discuss the thoughts presented, and
- prayers.

This smorgasbord approach gives you options for your mood, your family's mood, how much time you have, and how deep you want to go. My prayer is that whatever combination of thoughts you read from this book, individually or with your family, it would assist the Holy Spirit in making *The 25 Days of Christmas* as special as you have ever experienced.

—GREG JOHNSON

The Life of Our Lord for My Dear Children

CHARLES DICKENS

Charles Dickens is best remembered for authoring A Christmas Carol, *a novel made into many movies that families have enjoyed for decades. But he was also a Christian who had the same desire as any father: "Make sure that the children I am responsible to shepherd understand and accept the true meaning of Jesus." This opening selection reminds us once again how precious the Lord has been through the centuries, and that the "old, old story" is still fresh and new today.*

I am very anxious that you should know something about the history of Jesus Christ. For everyone ought to know about Him. No one ever lived who was so good, so kind, so gentle, and so sorry for all people who did wrong, or were in any way as ill or miserable as He was. And as He is now in Heaven, where we hope to go, and all to meet each other after we are dead, and there be happy always together, you never can think what a good place Heaven is, without knowing who He was and what He did.

He was born a long, long time ago—nearly two thousand years ago—at a place called Bethlehem. His father and mother lived in a city called Nazareth, but they were forced by business to travel to Bethlehem. His father's name was Joseph, and His mother's name was Mary. And the town being very full of people, also brought there by business, there was no room for Joseph and Mary in the inn or in any house; so they went into a stable to lodge, and in this stable Jesus Christ was born. There was no cradle or anything of that kind there, so Mary lay her pretty little boy in what is called a manger, which is a place the horses eat out of. And there He fell asleep.

Prologue

While He was asleep, some shepherds who were watching sheep in the fields saw an angel from God, all light and beautiful, come moving over the grass towards them. At first they were afraid and fell down and hid their faces. But the angel said, "There is a child born today in the city of Bethlehem near here. He will grow up and teach men to love one another, and not to quarrel and hurt one another; and His name will be Jesus Christ." And then the angel told the shepherds to go to that stable, and look at that little child in the manger. Which they did; and they kneeled down by Him in His sleep, and said, "God bless this child."[1]

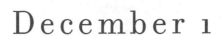

December 1

Today's Scripture:

John 1:14

The Word became a human and lived among us. We saw his glory—the glory that belongs to the only Son of the Father—and he was full of grace and truth.

Suggested Longer Readings:

John 1:1–14 *and* **Hebrews 1:1–3**

Avner and the Morning Star

ANGELA ELWELL HUNT

When God created the earth and space, he flung billions of stars through the velvet heavens. Upon each star he placed an angel. "Now I will create man," God told the angels. "Each time a baby is born, one of you will leave your star to guard the child. You will keep him safe from harm for as long as he wants my help."

Avner sighed. He waited on a shy little star, a nearly-nothing nova far from earth. *I may be on a tiny star,* he thought, *but I will train to be the mightiest guardian angel in God's service.*

Avner practiced zipping through space until he could fly to the sun and back a billion times in a second. He sat in the very center of his blazing star until he was sure he could withstand the heat of Satan's fiery darts. He built up his angelic muscles by hurling asteroids through space.

While Avner readied himself, boys and girls were born on earth, and people filled the planet. Thousands of guardian angels were already busy.

"Whew," Rigel whispered to Avner as he flew by. "I've just spent weeks guiding Abraham's servant toward Rebekah, God's chosen bride for Isaac."

I am faster than Rigel, thought Avner. *I could have brought Abraham's servant to Rebekah in the single beat of a human heart.*

Another night Altair whizzed by. "What an adventure!" he called. "I've just saved Shadrach, Meshach, and Abednego from a blazing furnace!"

I could have saved them from a hundred furnaces, thought Avner. *The feeble fires of earth are nothing like the terrible heat of my star.*

"Greetings!" Sirius called to Avner one morning. "I've just saved the prophet Daniel. I grappled with hungry lions and held their mouths closed all night!"

I could have shut their mouths with my little finger, Avner thought, flexing his muscles. *So why doesn't God send me to serve a child of earth?*

Finally an angel captain summoned Avner to the throne room of heaven, where the archangels Michael and Gabriel knelt before God. "It is time for Gabriel to visit the girl called Mary," God said. "The birth of her child will bring great joy and great trouble."

"I can guard her child," Avner volunteered, stepping boldly into the light of God's holiness. "I can protect a child from anything."

Michael smiled. "You will be called when it is time," he told Avner. "Go to your star and wait."

As he waited, Avner zipped impatiently around his star. His powerful speed made the star spin faster and burn hotter. Just when he thought it would shine brighter than the earth's sky, he heard God's voice: "Go. The child will be born in Bethlehem."

As Avner's star blazed overhead in the Bethlehem night, Mary's child was born. In the first instant Avner gazed upon the boy's face, he knew this was no ordinary baby. The love and wisdom in the child's eyes had existed long before earth. Avner began to tremble. God had asked him to safeguard the only Son of God.

While Avner hovered invisibly above the newborn Jesus, he heard other angel voices shout the wonderful news. Now all creation must have heard that God existed in a tiny, helpless baby. Avner spread his protective wings wider over the man and woman who watched the babe in the manger.

Avner's bright star brought the first serious trouble. Men from the East followed it in search of the newborn King, and they stopped to ask jealous King Herod for news. Avner appeared to Joseph in a dream and sped the young family out of Bethlehem just before Herod's soldiers killed every baby boy in the city.

Great joy and great trouble, Avner thought, remembering what God had said, *'Tis a good thing that Jesus has a fast guardian angel.*

Jesus's family settled in Nazareth, and Avner blinked in amazement when the one who had filled the universe with his presence, first took three wobbly steps in a fragile human body. He marveled that one who had commanded billions of powerful angels obeyed a poor man and woman. He was astonished when the one who had spoken the world into existence skinned his knee and ran to his mother for comfort.

Avner watched over Jesus for many years. When Jesus was ready to begin his work, he went into the wilderness to pray. For forty days he did not eat, and he grew hungry, lonely, and tired.

When Jesus was at his weakest, Satan and his army approached. Avner unsheathed his blade of light.

"Put your sword away," Jesus said.

Avner slowly lowered his weapon while Satan's army giggled. They parted to make way for their wicked master, who furiously attacked Jesus. Pleasure, money, and power would be his, the devil promised, if Jesus would obey Satan instead of God.

Jesus lifted his weary eyes and refused the devil's temptation. Satan howled in fury and fled, and Avner moved in to shelter Jesus from the rain of fiery darts from Satan's retreating army.

Great joy and great trouble, Avner thought, as his wings withstood the flaming arrows. *'Tis a good thing Jesus has a fireproof guardian angel.*

One night Jesus went to a garden with three of his closest friends. Jesus knelt in prayer, but his friends went to sleep. "Father, if you are willing, take this choice from me," Jesus prayed, as great drops of sweat rolled down his forehead. "But I want whatever you want."

"Why are you so sad?" Avner asked, appearing next to Jesus. "I am strong enough to protect you."

"You don't understand," Jesus answered. "You are an angel and will live forever. I must find strength enough to die."

"No!" Avner cried, slashing the clouds with his sword of light. The heavens rumbled in protest.

"Put down your sword," Jesus whispered. "Tonight I need a strong friend."

While the disciples slept, Avner sat with Jesus. *Great joy and great trouble*, he thought, a protective feeling rising inside him. *'Tis a good thing Jesus has a strong guardian angel.*

The sound of approaching footsteps halted Jesus's prayer. "Go," Jesus said, and Avner vanished. As the angel watched from the night sky, Jesus put out his hands. Soldiers bound him and led him away.

Avner watched in horror as Jesus stood alone before cruel men who had long forgotten God. Angels on distant stars covered their faces in shame and fear as the Son of God walked down a dusty street to be crucified.

Avner flew to the throne room of heaven. "Surely it is time to act!" he cried to God. "Let me annihilate those who would do this to your Son! With one stroke of my sword I could destroy them all, for I am the mightiest guardian angel!"

"No," God answered. "I did not send my Son into the world to destroy mankind."

Gabriel lifted his anguished face. "The Son of God carries the sin of the world," he said. "Return to your star and wait."

From far away Avner heard all creation groan as Jesus died. The angels covered the sun and stars with their wings, the heavens wore black in mourning. But on earth, most men and women went on as if nothing had happened.

Avner drifted back to his star, now gleaming blood red in the sky. *Great trouble and great sorrow,* he thought miserably. *And I am a great failure.*

After three sad days, Michael appeared before Avner. "Go to the tomb where they laid Jesus," the archangel commanded. "Roll away the stone you will find there."

Avner zipped to the tomb in a second, and one tap of his finger pushed the huge stone aside. The tomb was empty.

Suddenly Jesus stood beside him, and Avner fell to his knees. "Tell those who will come here that sin and death are defeated," Jesus said. "Not by might, but by love, mankind has been redeemed."

In a flash of understanding, Avner realized that Jesus did not want him to be creation's mightiest guardian angel. He wanted Avner to love man as much as he did.

"Yes," Jesus said, knowing Avner's thoughts. "Through great joy and great trouble, I love the people of earth. In the days to come, many will choose to follow me."

"How can I help them?" Avner whispered.

Jesus smiled. "The angel army needs a captain," he said. "A mighty and loving guardian angel."

When God created the earth and space, he flung billions of stars through the velvet heavens. Upon each star he placed an angel, and the single shining star that lingers until morning is Avner's. He's so busy taking care of God's people, you see, that he sometimes forgets to put the light out.[1]

Family Moment

Jesus is the message of Christmas. There has never been anyone else like him. And forgiveness for our sins is the central message of his birth and life on earth, his death on the cross, and especially his resurrection.

Ask family members what makes Jesus special to them.

An Advent Prayer

Lord, we thank you for being our Wonderful Counselor, Mighty God, Everlasting Father, and Prince of Peace. As we enter the Christmas season, give us grace that we may cast away the works of darkness. As you sent your messengers, the prophets, to prepare the way of salvation, may we prepare traditions that nurture our spiritual lives and celebrate the dawning of your everlasting light. In Jesus's name, amen.

More Meaning
by Joe Wheeler

Our family began each season, as did the early church, with the season of the Advent. Around the first of December, we turned off the television set and left it off for thirty-six days. In the place of television, we set up as the focal center of our lives a manger scene, or crèche. We posted an Advent calendar and planned family activities that reflected on the spiritual dimensions of the season. . . We took the family to attend sacred concerts, oratorios, and pageants. All the jolly commercial Santa Clauses were traded in for the self-giving spirit of St. Nicholas. Whenever possible, we visited and served those less fortunate than ourselves. Each evening during the days of Advent, we gathered around the fireside, shared Christmas stories, sang Christmas music, and fellowshipped with our extended family.

December 2

Today's Scripture:

Philippians 2:11

And everyone will confess that Jesus Christ is Lord and bring glory to God the Father.

Suggested Longer Readings:

Philippians 2:5–11 *and* **Romans 12:9–21**

The Christmas Room

GILLETTE JONES

Joan's family was the wealthiest in town, Barbara's one of the poorest. But one thing Joan's family didn't have was a Christmas room. So she came over to see. Would she ridicule it? Would she sneer? Would she laugh?

When I arrived at my daughter's on Christmas Eve, the children ran to the door with shouts and kisses, giving me a greeting that would make any grandma glad. Then, struggling with my bags, they took me to the guest room. I stopped short at the door of the room, staring at the sign that hung there. In red and green crayon it read: The Christmas Room. My throat ached for a moment, as I remembered. . . .

Our daughter, Barbara, was only nine when she began to realize we were quite poor. In Barbara's class was one girl who took special delight in tormenting her. It was an odd friendship between Barbara and Joan. Joan came from the wealthiest family in town, one of the few that hadn't been affected by the Depression. Joan was outgoing, Barbara quiet and shy.

Joan was all ups and downs: one minute befriending Barbara, treating her to candy, giving her a toy—the next, bragging extravagantly, teaching Barbara to be ashamed of our house.

We kept hoping Barbara would overcome her shyness and make other friends, but she continued to tag after Joan, in spite of the hurts she suffered. Joan, delighting in Barbara's vulnerability, kept her on a string at her side.

Christmas was coming. I knew ours would be a lean one indeed unless we used a great deal of imagination. Early in November we started planning. Barbara helped me look for recipes that were inexpensive. We colored Epson salts and put it in pretty bottles for bath salts for her grandmothers. We took scraps of velvet and transformed ordinary boxes into jewel boxes for the grandfathers' stickpins. We spent hours in the little spare room, laughing at each new touch of imagination.

The lumpy old daybed became littered with gay scraps of paper as we cut pictures from last year's Christmas cards to decorate our packages. We had a wonderful time together.

One day in early December, Barbara went to Joan's house after school and returned looking sad.

"What's the trouble?" I asked her.

"Oh, nothing."

"There is something," I said. "Is Joan bragging again?"

"It's not that. I'm sort of used to that." She hesitated, then said, "Mom, I told a fib today."

I was thankful she found it disturbing, at least.

"But that Joan!" Her voice had an edge of bitterness. "She's always talking about the Blue Room and the company who sleeps there. Today she asked me, 'Where does your company sleep?'"

We never had overnight company. It was hard enough to feed ourselves on Jim's meager salary. And our homely little spare room was just that. It had two old pieces of furniture in it—a daybed and a wobbly end table.

Barbara went on. "I told Joan we don't have much company, and her eyebrow went up. Mom, I just couldn't stand that look again. So I told her, 'We have something you don't. We have a Christmas room.'"

Her feet shuffled. "I didn't mean to fib, but you should have seen how surprised she looked. I never saw Joan stuck before. She really didn't know what to say."

"But dear, you weren't fibbing," I said. "We do have a Christmas room. But if it will make it more official, we'll make a sign for the door."

She brightened. "Oh, could we?"

"We'll do it today."

The sign was barely dry and hung when Joan arrived. She had rarely come to our house, always preferring to take Barbara to her house, where there were lots of toys to play with. Now she stood at our door, asking to see the Christmas room.

Barbara looked at me. "May I show her?"

"I guess so," I answered. "If everything is wrapped, that is." Barbara went to check on the condition of packages while I explained to Joan, "The room is full of surprises and we can't let any secrets out."

Barbara hurried back into the room. "It's OK."

I held my breath. Joan would see only a small, dingy room with a cracked ceiling and a homemade sign on the door. She would not see or feel the special qualities that room held for us.

They were gone so long I finally went into the hallway and peered in. Joan was looking at our crèche—paper figures we had cut and stood on the end table.

"We have china figures," she said. "Imported."

I started to speak but just then Joan moved to the packages that were lined up on the daybed. She touched them, one by one, lingering over the one with the paper sled on it. That was one Barbara had done from colored paper. She had filled the sled with miniature packages.

Joan turned to Barbara. "We don't have surprises. I always know everything."

"How?" Barbara asked. "Do you peek?"

Joan shook her had. "They ask what I want—and I get it."

Barbara said impulsively, "I'll give you a surprise."

Joan shrugged. "If you want."

Barbara nodded solemnly, before I could stop her.

During the next week we tossed ideas about, rejecting them all. There seemed nothing we could give this child who had everything. At last we settled somewhat apprehensively on giving her one afternoon a week at our house, helping to make surprises. I wasn't at all sure she'd think it was a present.

She did come, however. The first time we made cookies and wrapped some for her mother. The next week it was fancy matchboxes for her father. The week before Christmas Barbara gave her a box to open. Joan tore at the paper, but when she had the lid off she didn't know what the contents were. Barbara looked disappointed, and I added, "It's corn—for popping."

I tried to force gaity into my words. It wasn't easy when Barbara's face said plainly that she wished we had given Joan something different, something better.

When the corn was popped, Joan tasted it and remarked, "I could never make this. It's too messy for our house."

I glanced quickly at Barbara, but she was busy showing Joan how the corn could be dyed pink or blue with food coloring.

"Later, we'll string it for the Christmas tree," she explained.

Joan worked at it, occasionally holding up the colorful string without comment. I couldn't tell whether she was having fun. But suddenly I knew I wanted her to—very much.

"They'll never hang this on our tree," she snorted.

"Would you like to come hang it on our tree?" I ventured.

Her sudden tears alarmed me. "Could I?" she asked. "I can never help trim ours. I might break things." She pushed back her chair. "I'd better go now."

She got her coat and hat quickly, but in the Christmas room she had a long moment of hesitation about whether to actually take home the things she'd made for her parents. At last she decided. She picked them up.

We watched her leave, clutching her small surprises. Both of us hoped that her parents would not laugh at her offerings.

Barbara turned big eyes toward me and whispered, "I used to be jealous of her."

That was long ago, when Barbara was very young. It had been a childhood thing, important at the time but long forgotten, I'd thought. Now once again I stood facing a sign on a door that read, The Christmas Room.

I stepped into a pleasant room with pale-blue walls and crisp curtains, not at all like our homely old spare room. On the window seat there were packages wrapped with special touches of childish imagination.

The children ran to them.

"I made this!" Ronnie cried proudly.

"You're going to love mine, Grandma," Paula shouted.

There was no financial need for Barbara to do with her children what we had done—but I was so glad she had. She'd been young that year of the Christmas room, yet even then she must have known that a Christmas room is a room for people, for thoughts of others, a room in the heart.[1]

∞

Family Moment

It's hard to imagine all that Jesus left when he put aside his majestic robes and arrived on this planet as an humble servant. Have family members try to make a comparison of what that would be like for them—to leave the comfort of their lives for other places. Ask them to describe their lives today, and then imagine themselves in a place where all that was gone.

How tough was that to do? Why is it hard to imagine doing that?

An Advent Prayer

Lord, Jesus. You left heaven and the place beside your Father to come to earth . . . to rescue us. That is almost too unbelievable to believe. You did it not to prove some point about how much better you were, but for the love of each individual that was ever born, including me. I thank you today for the example of humility you have given me. Help me never to be so proud of my home and possessions that I forget how you invaded our world by choice so that we would have the choice of loving you from the deepest part of our hearts. In his name, amen.

More Meaning

Don't view the Christmas holidays as one long season. Instead, vow to enjoy every little facet of it for yourself. For example, make gift wrapping a total experience in itself, rather than a chore that you must accomplish before some self-imposed deadline. In addition, vow to appreciate rather than depreciate all activities, including shopping, card writing with the children, decorating with everyone involved, and meal preparation.

Be spontaneous in each of these activities as well as creatively original. Make each thing you do fun and an experience unto itself, instead of one big headache that has many unbearable component parts. That's precisely how children approach everything in the Christmas season. Cookie making, stocking stuffing, caroling, wrapping presents, decorating, and so on, are all individual fun things to the children, and can be for you as well.[2]

—W. Dyer

December 3

Today's Scripture:

2 Corinthians 5:20

So we have been sent to speak for Christ. It is as if God is calling to you through us. We speak for Christ when we beg you to be at peace with God.

Suggested Longer Readings:

2 Kings 7:1−9 *and* **2 Corinthians 5:17−20**

The Parable of the Shopper

AUTHOR UNKNOWN

My feet were tired, my hands cold, my arms exhausted from the weight of the packages, and it was beginning to snow. The bus was late. I kept rearranging my packages, trying to hold them in a different way in order to give my poor arms a rest. I still remember that day as if it were yesterday, and yet fifteen years have gone by. Nevertheless, when Christmas rolls around, I remember that day on the bus.

I was tired. I had been Christmas shopping all day long. When the bus finally arrived, it was packed with holiday shoppers in the same exhausted mood as I. I sank into the only vacant place, near the back, by a handsome gentleman. He politely helped me to situate my packages and even held some of them himself.

"My goodness," he said, "did you leave any merchandise still in the stores for the rest of us?"

"I don't think so," I moaned. "Worst of all, I still haven't made all of my purchases."

The woman in the seat behind us joined in my grief and added, "No, the worst thing is that the day after Christmas we will be carrying this same arm-load back to the store to exchange it."

Her comment brought a general chuckle from all those within earshot, including my seat mate. As the laughter subsided, he began in a quiet, melodious voice, deepened with experience, to teach me a lesson that I have never forgotten:

"Hear now the parable of the shopper," he said, speaking gently and indicating my packages. "A woman went forth to shop, and as she shopped, she carefully planned. Each child's desires were considered. The hard-earned money was divided, and the many purchases were made with the pure joy and delight that is known only to the giver. Then the girfts were wrapped and placed lovingly under the tree. In eager anticipation she scanned each face as the gifts were opened."

" 'What a lovely sweater,' said the eldest daughter, 'but I think I would prefer blue. I suppose I can exchange it?'

" 'Thank you for the cassette player, Mother. It's just what I wanted,' said her son. And then aside, secretly to his sister, he continued, 'I told her I wanted the one with the automatic reverse and an extra speaker. I never get what I want!'

"The youngest child spoke out with the spoiled honesty of her age, 'I hate rag dolls! I wanted a china doll. I won't play with it!' And the doll, still in the box, was kicked under the couch."

"One gift still lay under the tree. The woman pointed it out to her husband. 'Your gift is still there.'

" 'I'll open it when I have the time,' he stated. 'I want to get this bike put together first.'

"How sad it is," continued his soft, beautiful voice. "When gifts are not received in the same spirit they are given. To reject a thoughtful gift is to reject the loving sentiment of the giver himself. And yet, are we not all sometimes guilty of rejecting?"

He was talking not only to me, but to all of those on the bus. They had all gathered around. The bus was parked.

He took a present from my stack.

"This one," he said, holding it up and pretending to open the card, "could be to you." He pointed to a rough-looking, teenage boy in a worn denim jacket and pretended to read the gift card. "To you I give My life, lived perfectly, as an example so that you might see the pattern and live worthy to return and live with Me again. Merry Christmas from the Messiah."

"This one," he said, holding up a pure, white present, "is for you." He held out the gift to a worn-looking woman, who in earlier years must have been a real beauty. She read the card out loud and allowed her tears to slip without shame down her painted face. "My gift to you is repentance. This Christmas I wish you to know for certain that though your sins be as scarlet, they shall be white as snow. Signed, your Advocate with the Father."

"That isn't all. No, here is a big, red package." he looked around the group and brought a ragged, unkempt, little child forward. "This package would be for you if He were here. The card would say, 'On this Christmas and always, My gift to you is love. From your brother, Jesus.'"

"One final gift," said my seat mate. "The greatest of all the gifts of God—Eternal life!"

He held our minds and our hearts. We were a hungry audience. Though our shopping had left us drained, now we were being filled by his words.

"How we receive these gifts, these precious gifts from the Babe of Bethlehem, is the telling point. Are we exchangers?" he asked. "Is there really anything else we would rather have? It is what we do with a gift long after we have opened it that shows our true appreciation."

With those words he was gone. That was fifteen years ago, only a wink in time. But not even an eternity could erase the sermon, or the man.[1]

Family Moment

We hear so often the phrase "Jesus died for me" that sometimes we forget the purpose of salvation isn't just to be glad our souls are safe for eternity; it's to follow Jesus's example—give ourselves to others. That's what the Scripture talks about in 2 Kings, and that's what Christ did for us.

The truth is, we were saved *from* something *for* something.

As a family, you can create a giving experience by going to a homeless shelter or making sandwiches to pass out, and this is a good thing to do. But what if this year you prayed for God to send a giving experience? God is more than able to answer and would delight at your willingness to be a blessing in the life of another soul—or many souls—whom he loves.

An Advent Prayer

Our Father in heaven, thank you for being the gift that holds families together, even over time and distance. Is there someone I know who needs the present and the presence of Jesus in their home this Christmas? Is there a stranger? Please show me who. I want more than ever to give your love to those who need it. You gave yourself for me when I needed it. Help me to do the same. In the name of Jesus, amen

December 4

Today's Scripture:

Isaiah 9:6

> *A child has been born to us; God has given a son to us. He*
> *will be responsible for leading the people. His name will*
> *be Wonderful Counselor, Powerful God, Father Who Lives*
> *Forever, Prince of Peace.*

Suggested Longer Readings:

Isaiah 9:1–7 *and* Psalm 139:13–18

17

In Another Stable

DAVID NIVEN

This story is written by David Niven, the famous actor from years ago who appeared in more than sixty movies.

It took place on Christmas Eve 1939. I had just arrived in England from Hollywood to volunteer for the British Army. Having had some previous military experience, I was commissioned a second lieutenant and given command of a platoon. We were about to be sent to France, and no one was very happy about it. Most of the men had been conscripted from good civilian jobs; this was the "phony war" period before the big German attack of the following spring, and it all seemed a big waste of time to most of them.

Being commanded by a Hollywood actor was an additional irritant for them and made the whole thing seem even more ridiculous. The men were not mutinous, but they were certainly forty of the least well-disposed characters I ever have been associated with, let alone been in command of.

We were not permitted liberty on that Christmas Eve because we were due to leave England and our families the next day—a fine prospect for the holidays. The entire platoon was billeted in the shabby stables of a farm near Dover.

I could sense the hostility in every soldier. The air was thick with sarcastic cracks about my bravery in various motion pictures.

It so happens that every night of my life I have knelt down by my bed and said a simple prayer. But that night I was faced with a difficult decision. If I suddenly knelt in prayer, here in front of these men, it occurred to me that forty tough soldiers would take it as a final evidence of Hollywood flamboyance.

On the other hand, I have always felt it wrong to avoid saying my prayers because the situation was not convenient. Besides, here it was the eve of Christ's birth.

Finally I summoned up my courage and knelt by my bunk. As I prayed there was some snickering at first, but it soon died away.

When I finished and lay down on the straw, I looked rather sheepishly around the stable and saw at least a dozen soldiers kneeling quietly and praying in their own way.

It was not the first time God had entered a stable—and touched the hearts of men.[1]

Family Moment

During this season we are to look for and serve the Christ in others. We are to think of others before we think of ourselves, that is, we are "to walk in another's shoes." Our family best implemented this by having Secret Angels for the four weeks of Christmas. As the angel, we tried to look at things the way the person whose name we had drawn would. This included looking at the hardships and perhaps the duties he or she had to do, as well as the experiences that would gladden the heart and delight the spirit. When one chooses an angel, one takes on the responsibility to treat that person in a very special, thoughtful way.

To choose secret angels, put each name on a slip of paper, and then let each person take a name—not his or her own, of course. It is important to keep the name a secret until a set time when all of you can share whom you have been serving. Some families might choose to reveal the angel at Christmas Eve supper or Christmas morning at the breakfast table. It could be done by putting the angel's name on a slip of paper and tucking it under the plate. Everyone could look at the same time. In our family we hang stockings. The angel stuffs the stocking and reveals his or her name at that time.

The Secret Angels in our family have done many and varied services. We have shined shoes or cleaned a pair of boots, set tables, and fed animals when it was not our turn. Before we had a garage door opener, opening the garage for Dad was a welcome he cherished. Often we have found bed covers turned back and slippers and nightclothes laid out in a tidy fashion. Above all, remember these are acts of service. We serve each other by trying to determine what would help the other person.

Maybe there won't be surprises every day, but there ought to be enough in a week's time to assure each family member that he or she does, indeed, have an angel and that the angel is watching him or her with interest.

An Advent Prayer

Father God in heaven, our human ability to uncover all of the ways you are wonderful seems to fall short. We try to understand, sometimes we think we understand, but our efforts at truly grasping why you love us, why you came to earth, why you lived a sinless life and died a criminal's death . . . for one like me . . . perhaps there are no words. But Jesus, in this quiet moment in my heart, our hearts, we just want to say, "You're wonderful! Wonderful in more ways than we can say. You're wonderful today, and we look forward to all of the tomorrows you give us to discover even more how wonderful you are." In your name, amen.

Christmas Facts

Gift Giving

The first Christmas gifts were those brought by the three wise men to the newborn Jesus at Bethlehem. The symbolic exchange of gifts at Christmastime, the world over, reflects the spirit of the gift-bearing Magi.

Hark! The Herald Angels Sing

Charles Wesley

Felix Mendelssohn

Brightly

1. Hark! the her - ald an - gels sing, __ Glo - ry to the new - born King;

Peace on earth, and mer - cy mild, __ God and sin - ners rec - on - ciled!

Joy - ful all ye na - tions, rise, __ Join the tri - umph of the skies; __

With th' an - gel -ic host pro - claim, Christ is __ born in Beth - le - hem.

Refrain

Hark! the her - ald an - gels sing, Glo - ry __ to the new - born King.

The hinge of history
is on the
door
of a Bethlehem
stable.

—RALPH W. SOCKMAN

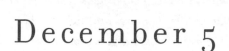

December 5

Today's Scripture:

Isaiah 55:8–9

The Lord says, "My thoughts are not like your thoughts.
Your ways are not like my ways. Just as the heavens are
higher than the earth, so are my ways higher than your
ways and my thoughts higher than your thoughts."

Suggested Longer Readings:

Isaiah 55:6–9 *and* **Hebrews 11:1–6**

To See Again

GARY B. SWANSON

> We all take our senses for granted, placing, instead, undue value on monetary things. We'd be happy, we say, if Publisher's Clearing House made us multi-millionaires. But multimillionaires are rarely very happy, so something must be wrong with that assertion. This little story reminds us that some things dwarf mere money.

The mother sat on the simulated-leather chair in the doctor's office, picking nervously at her fingernail. Wrinkles of worry lined her forehead as she watched five-year-old Kenny sitting on the rug before her.

He was small for his age and a little too thin, she thought. His fine blond hair hung down smooth and straight to the top of his ears. But white gauze bandages encircled his head, covering his eyes and pinning his ears back.

In his lap he bounced a beaten-up teddy bear. It was the pride of his life, yet one arm was gone and the other missing. Twice his mother had tried to throw it away and replace it with a new one, but he had fussed, so she had relented. She tipped her head slightly to the side and smiled at him. *It's really about all he has,* she sighed to herself.

A nurse appeared in the doorway. "Kenny," she announced, and the young mother scooped him up and followed the nurse toward the examining room. The hallway smelled of rubbing alcohol and bandages. Children's crayon drawings lined the walls.

"The doctor will be with you in a moment," the nurse said with an efficient smile. "Please be seated."

The mother placed Kenny on the examining table. "Be careful, honey, not to fall off."

"Am I up very high, Mother?"

"No, dear, but be careful."

Kenny hugged his teddy bear tighter. "Then I don't want Grr-face to fall either."

The mother smiled. The smile twisted at the corners into a frown of concern. She brushed the hair of the boy's face and caressed his cheek, soft as thistledown, with the back of her hand. As the music drifted into a haunting version of "Silent Night," she remembered the accident for the thousandth time.

She had been cooking things on the back burner for years. But there it was, sitting right out in front, water almost boiling for oatmeal.

The phone rang in the living room. It was another one of those "free offers" that cost so much. At the moment she returned the phone to the table, Kenny screamed in the kitchen, the galvanizing cry of pain that frosts a mother's veins.

She winced again at the memory of it and brushed aside a warm tear slipping down her cheek. Six weeks they had waited for this day to come. "We'll be able to take the bandages off the week before Christmas," the doctor had said.

The door to the examination room swept open, and Dr. Harris came in. "Good morning, Mrs. Ellis," he said brightly. "How are you today?"

"Fine, thank you," she said. But she was too apprehensive for small talk.

Dr. Harris bent over the sink and washed his hands carefully. He was cautious with his patients but careless about himself. He could seldom find time to get a haircut, and his straight black hair hung a little long over his collar. His loosened tie allowed his collar to be open at the throat.

"Now then," he said, sitting down on a stool, "let's have a look."

Gently he snipped at the bandage with scissors and unwound it from Kenny's head. The bandage fell away, leaving two flat squares of gauze taped directly over Kenny's eyes. Dr. Harris lifted the edges of the tape slowly, trying not to hurt the boy's tender skin.

Kenny slowly opened his eyes and blinked several times as if the sudden light hurt. Then he looked at his mother and grinned. "Hi, Mom," he said.

Choking and speechless, the mother threw her arms around Kenny's neck. For several minutes she could say nothing, as she hugged the boy and wept in thankfulness. Finally, she looked at Dr. Harris with tear-filled eyes. "I don't know how we'll ever be able to pay you," she said. "Since my husband died it's been hard for us."

"We've been over all that before," the doctor interrupted with a wave of his hand. "I know how this is for you and Kenny. I'm glad I could help."

The mother dabbed at her eyes with a welcome handkerchief, stood up, and took Kenny's hand. And just as she turned toward the door Kenny pulled up and stood for a long moment looking uncertainly at the doctor. Then he held his teddy bear up by its only arm to the doctor.

"Here," he said, "take my Grr-face. He ought to be worth a lot of money."

Dr. Harris quietly took the broken bear in his hands. "Thank you, Kenny. This will more than pay for my services."

The last few days before Christmas were especially good for Kenny and his mother. They sat together through the long evenings, watching the Christmas tree twinkle on and off. Bandages had covered Kenny's eyes for six weeks, so he seemed reluctant to close them to sleep at night. The fire dancing in the fireplace, snowflakes sticking to his bedroom window, the small packages under the tree—all the lights of the holiday fascinated him.

And then, on Christmas Eve, Kenny's mother answered the doorbell. No one was there, but a large package was on the porch, wrapped in metallic green paper with a broad red ribbon and bow. A tag attached to the package identified the box as intended for Kenny Ellis.

With a grin, Kenny tore the ribbon off the box, lifted the lid, and pulled out a teddy bear—his beloved Grr-face. Only it now had a new arm of brown corduroy and two new button eyes that glittered in the soft Christmas light. Kenny didn't seem to mind that the new arm did not match the other one. He just hugged the teddy bear and laughed.

Among the tissue in the box, the mother found a card. "Dear Kenny," it read, "I can sometimes help put boys and girls back together, but Mrs. Harris had to help me repair Grr-face. She's a better bear doctor than I am. Merry Christmas! Dr. Harris."

"Look, Mother," Kenny smiled, pointing to the button eyes. "Grr-face can see again—just like me!"[1]

Family Moment

On a scale of one to ten, ask family members where they stand on the invisible "trust meter." If the people who are telling them biblical truth are credible, can they believe something that seems out of the ordinary? Or are they the type who must have proof about everything; does every fact have to be confirmed scientifically before they can believe?

It's a fact that it's easier for some to have faith in stories they've not seen or experienced personally. Why? Because they trust the storyteller.

As a family, name some things you trust in daily life that you cannot see (Hints: wind, electricity, the mail being delivered, Mom making healthy preparations of food, Dad locking the doors at night). Come up with as many as you can imagine—make the list long!

Are any facts in the Bible hard to trust? Give permission to all family members to mention anything they want. Fight the urge to try to "prove" anything unless it seems warranted; just take it in and tuck it away for a later conversation. Your children need to know they can express questions and doubts without sermons to correct them.

An Advent Prayer

Dear Lord, I admit that I do not understand all of the reasons why you had to come to show us you were both God and man. But I'm glad you did. I'm thankful that you were human, so you understand all of my weaknesses and fears. You experienced them all. And I'm thankful that you are fully God. You are not just another counselor with human wisdom; you are incarnate wisdom for my life. You are able to come to my aid in the supernatural ways that I need. This is amazing. You are amazing. Bless you, Lord Jesus, for being willing to invade this world to help a human such as me see the light of eternity. Amen.

More Meaning

Slow yourself down when shopping for holiday gifts. Make the experience of shopping and being out in the world something you enjoy for itself, rather than a necessary barrier you must overcome on your way to having a nice holiday. Try to keep in mind how much you loved doing your holiday shopping as a child, then stop to say something kind to a harried sales clerk, sit and watch the people, ask questions about the new toys and electronic gadgets on the market, give some money to the charity collector, slow down and enjoy the scents of Christmas trees and wreaths, just as you did as a child. Give yourself permission to enjoy *all* aspects of this holiday season. When you take away the pace and go out into the world to shop and enjoy everything that you are going to encounter in the day, you'll have a set of expectations, even as you leave the house, that will permit you to enjoy everything you will do in the day. A day of shopping is going to be dreadful, only if *you* set out anticipating it to be that way.[2]

—W. Dyer

Good news from heaven
The angels bring,
Glad tidings to the earth they sing:
To us this day a
Child is given,
To crown us with
The joy of heaven.

— MARTIN LUTHER

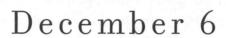

December 6

Today's Scripture:

Isaiah 52:7

How beautiful is the person who comes over the mountains to bring good news, who announces peace and brings good news, who announces salvation and says to Jerusalem, "Your God is King."

Suggested Longer Reading:

Isaiah 52:7–10

Now I Understand, Now I See Why

LOUIS CASSELS

> Some people have a big problem figuring out why God had to become a
> man to save the world from its sin. This is one of my all-time-favorite modern-
> day parables that explains the reason beautifully. Years ago, this story
> was made into a short cartoon that appeared in prime-time TV.

Once upon a time, there was man who looked upon Christmas as a lot of
humbug. He wasn't a scrooge. He was a very kind and decent person, gener-
ous to his family, upright in all his dealings with other men.

But he didn't believe all that stuff about the incarnation that churches
proclaim at Christmas. And he was too honest to pretend that he did.

"I am truly sorry to distress you," he told his wife, who was a faithful
churchgoer. "But I simply cannot understand this claim that God became
man. It doesn't make any sense to me."

On Christmas Eve, his wife and children went to church for the midnight
service. He declined to accompany them.

"I'd feel like a hypocrite," he explained. "I'd much rather stay at home.
But I'll wait up for you."

Shortly after his family drove away in the car, snow began to fall. He went
to the window and watched the flurries getting heavier and heavier.

"If we must have a Christmas," he reflected, "it's nice to have a white
one."

He went back to his chair by the fireside and began to read his newspaper.

A few minutes later, he was startled by a thudding sound. It was quickly
followed by another, then another. He thought that someone must be throw-
ing snowballs at the window.

When he went to the front door to investigate, he found a flock of birds
huddled miserably in the snow. They had been caught in the storm, and in a
desperate search for shelter had tried to fly through his window.

I can't let those poor creatures lie there and freeze, he thought. *But how can I help them?*

Then he remembered the barn where the children's pony was stabled. It would provide a warm shelter.

He quickly put on his coat and boots and tramped through the deepening snow to the barn. He opened the doors wide and turned on the light.

But the birds didn't come in.

Food will bring them in, he thought. So he hurried back to the house for bread crumbs, which he sprinkled on the snow to make a trail in the barn. To his dismay, the birds ignored the bread crumbs and continued to flop around helplessly in the snow.

He tried shooing them into the barn by walking around and waving his arms. They scattered in every direction—except into the warm, lighted barn.

They find me a strange and terrifying creature, he said to himself, *and I can't seem to think of any way to let them know they can trust me.*

If only I could be a bird myself for a few minutes, perhaps I could lead them to safety.

Just at that moment the church bells began to ring. He stood silently for a while, listening to the bells pealing the glad tidings of Christmas.

Then he sank to his knees in the snow.

"Now I understand," he whispered. "Now I see why you had to do it."[1]

Family Moment

The man in this story instinctively knew what it would take in order for the birds to be saved. Why? His thoughts were bigger, and his knowledge of fixing something like this more complete.

If you remember yesterday's scripture, you'll recall that God's thoughts are not even in our ability to understand. Our job? To trust that his plan—to become one of us in order to show us the way to eternal safety—is the best one.

Rack your brain for a moment. Put yourself in God's thoughts, and ask yourself questions like these:

I want to lead my creation whom I love to safety. What way can I show them, what method can I give them, in which they could all look to me for the direction they need?

Could all of the humans I created in my image go to church to find their way to eternal safety? Could they all give money? Could they all do good works? Could they all pray certain prayers for long periods of time, using just the right words to impress me? Could they all be born of a certain race? (Try to think of other ways people try to reach God.

The answer to all of these hypothetical questions is, of course, no. There is but one way that all could know and find his shelter.

Faith.

All can believe . . . if they hear.

An Advent Prayer

Heavenly Father, you saw us here on earth, bumping our heads and flapping around each in our own way. You looked at us with compassion and pondered what you could do to bring us to the safety and warmth of your arms. In your wisdom, you concluded that the only way we would really understand which direction to follow was to for you to become one of us. This you did. Thank you for sending your Son Jesus into this world so full of sin and hate and invading it with your love. You gave us your Word to show us the direction, and you gave us your Spirit to comfort our hearts and to give us confidence in our faith. All of this you did not only for the whole world, but you did it for me. All we can say is thank you. Amen.

December 7

Today's Scripture:

2 Corinthians 1:3

Praise be to the God and Father of our Lord Jesus Christ. God is the Father who is full of mercy and all comfort.

Suggested Longer Readings:

2 Corinthians 1:3–7 *and* **1 Corinthians 13:4–7**

If Christ Had Not Come

> A number of years ago a remarkable Christmas card was published by the title "If Christ Had Not Come." It was based on our Savior's own words, "If I had not come," in John 15:22. The card pictured a minister falling asleep in his study on Christmas morning and then dreaming of a world into which Jesus had never come.

In his dream, he saw himself walking through his house, but as he looked, he saw no stockings hung on the chimney, no Christmas tree, no wreaths of holly, and no Christ to comfort and gladden hearts or to save us. He then walked onto the street outside, but there was no church with its spire pointing toward heaven. And when he came back and sat down in his library, he realized that every book about our Savior had disappeared.

The minister dreamed that the doorbell rang and that a messenger asked him to visit a friend's poor dying mother. He reached her home, and as his friend sat and wept, he said, "I have something here that will comfort you." He opened his Bible to look for a familiar promise, but it ended with Malachi. There was no gospel and no promise of hope and salvation, and all he could do was bow his head and weep with his friend and his mother in bitter despair.

Two days later he stood beside her coffin and conducted her funeral service, but there was no message of comfort, no words of a glorious resurrection, and no thought of a mansion awaiting her in heaven. There was only, "dust to dust, and ashes to ashes," and one long eternal farewell. Finally he realized that *Christ had not come,* and burst into tears, weeping bitterly in his sorrowful dream.

Then suddenly he awoke with a start, and a great shout of joy and praise burst from his lips as he heard his choir singing these words in his church nearby:

O come, all ye faithful, joyful and triumphant,
O come ye, O come ye to Bethlehem!

Come and behold Him, born the King of angels,
O come let us adore Him, Christ the Lord!

Let us be glad and rejoice, because He *has* come. And let us remember the proclamation of the angel: "I bring you good news of great joy that will be *for all the people.* Today in the town of David a Savior has been born to you; he is Christ the Lord" (Luke 2:10–11 NIV, emphasis added).

He comes to make His blessing flow,
Far as the curse does go.

May our hearts go out to the unconverted people of foreign lands who have no blessed Christmas Day. "Go and enjoy choice food and sweet drinks, and *send some to those who have nothing prepared.* This day is sacred to our LORD" (Nehemiah 8:10 NIV, emphasis added).

Family Moment
Think about all of the traditions and Christian symbols you have in your life. Ask family members what they think life would be like without them.

Next, ask what each person would miss most about Jesus if he did not exist. What quality? What word of comfort? What word of truth? What story would be missed the most?

An Advent Prayer

Dear Father in heaven, even the thought that you didn't come into this world is hard to imagine. Through the people who call on your name, you have made much of the world a place where people are loved, where families can live in peace, where celebrating your birth is a privilege granted, not a gift unopened. For centuries, you have worked through those who serve you to be your representative of love here on earth. This Christmas season, work through each family member in this home to be an incarnation of your love to another when they least expect it, or when they most need it. We're a family, Lord, and we want to love each other as a family should. In Jesus's name, amen.

Christmas Facts

Christmas Greetings

The sending of Christmas cards seems to have originated in England about the middle of the nineteenth century. Queen Anne commissioned several famed artists to decorate their thoughts of holiday greetings. One of the first Christmas greetings was prepared for Queen Victoria by a man named Dobson, one of the queen's most treasured printers.

To Add Christmas Cheer

To add sparkle to your Christmas cards this year,
address and stamp all your holiday cards.
Put them in a large envelope and send them to
the postmaster in Santa Claus, Indiana,
or North Pole, New York.
Ask the postmaster to postmark them
from that town and mail them.
Your friends and family will love it!

O Come, All Ye Faithful

Old Latin Hymn

Majestically

1. O come, all ye faith - ful, Joy - ful and tri -
um - phant, O come ye, O come __ ye to Beth __ - le -
hem; Come and be - hold Him, Born the King of

Refrain

an __ - gels; O come, let us a - dore Him, O come, let us a -
dore Him, O come, let us a - dore Him, __ Christ, __ the Lord.

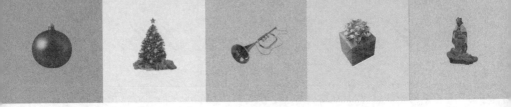

December 8

Today's Scripture:

Psalm 139:1

Lord, you have examined me and know all about me.

Suggested Longer Reading:

Psalm 139:1–12

A Boy's Finest Memory

CECIL B. DEMILLE

If you've seen The Ten Commandments, *the movie in which Charlton Heston plays Moses, you may remember Cecil B. DeMille. He was not only the director for the movie, he was the narrator. He directed several other biblical movies during his Hollywood years, and the reading below probably is one reason why. At an early age, he was exposed to something very real about Christianity: God accepts each human soul as if he or she were the only person with whom he had to deal.*

During this festive Christmas season, churches all over the country will overflow with worshipers. It wasn't always that way. . . .

When I was a boy of ten, our community church, in order to stimulate interest among parishioners, decided to hold services every morning at 8 a.m. for a week. Since we couldn't afford a resident minister, one was acquired from the outside. I do not remember his name. But I shall never forget his strong, kindly face and his prominent red beard.

My father, who was very active in the church, sent me off one cold and rainy morning. I walked alone to the small, wooden sanctuary through a murky gloom. Upon arriving, I could see that no one was present but the red-bearded minister and me.

I was the congregation.

Embarrassed, I took a seat, wondering anxiously what he would do. The hour for the service arrived. Surely he would tell me politely to run along home.

With calm and solemn dignity the minister walked into the pulpit. Then he looked down on me and smiled—a smile of great warmth and sincerity. In the congregation sat a solitary child, but he commenced the service as if the church were crowded to the walls.

A ritual opened the services, followed by a reading lesson to which I gave the responses. Then the minister preached a short sermon. He talked earnestly to me—and to God. When it came time for the offering, he placed the collection plate on the altar railing. I walked up and dropped my nickel into the plate.

Then he did a beautiful thing. He came down to the altar to receive my offering. As he did this, he placed his hand on my head. I can still feel the thrill and sensation of his gentle touch. It won my belief and strengthened my faith. The spirit of truth was in the church with us that morning.

None of us can tell at what moment we step into a boy's life and by a demonstration of love and faith turn him in God's direction.[1]

Family Moment

We are not just numbers to God. We aren't average faces in a sea of humanity that God looks down upon from a celestial abode.

We are unique creations of God whom Jesus personally died for on the cross. It's an awesome thought.

Ask family members if they feel they are special to God in any way. If yes, why? If no, why not? What more would God have to do in order to show them how loved and cherished they truly are to the God of creation? How could we show each other our love in practical ways?

An Advent Prayer

Father in heaven, once again, I'm confronted with the choice I have of either realizing how special I am to you, or somehow not believing that it is true. I understand that truly knowing this will be a process I must go through, but I want today to somehow feel something fresh and new about this truth. Show me through those who love me, show me through your Word, show me through an answered prayer, that you care deeply about me! I need this, Lord, in a world that doesn't seem to care too much. I need to hold tightly to the truth that you think I am special every moment of every day. In Jesus's name, amen.

More Meaning

Vow to yourself that you are going to find something to enjoy in every gift you receive. Also, decide that you are going to point out what you appreciate about the gift to the individual who took the time to think of you with a present. Forget about what the gift does for you, and remember that the real beauty of this particular gift is in the thoughtfulness a human being felt toward you. Force yourself to take an extra moment to say something nice to the giver, and stop thinking about how to return it, or why you don't like it, or having some other self-defeating reaction.[2]

Are you willing to believe that love is the strongest thing in the world—stronger than hate, stronger than evil, stronger than death—and that the blessed life which began in Bethlehem nineteen hundred years ago is the image and brightness of the Eternal Love? Then you can keep Christmas. And if you keep it for a day, why not always?

—HENRY VAN DYKE

December 9

Today's Scripture:

Luke 2:7

And she gave birth to her first son. Because there were no rooms left in the inn, she wrapped the baby with pieces of cloth and laid him in a box where animals are fed.

Suggested Longer Reading:

Luke 2:1–7

Trouble at the Inn

DINA DONOHUE

What could be new about a local nativity play? Children in bathrobes and sheets
flubbing their lines. . . . Not always. Sometimes this very spontaneity results in
the sudden need to wipe something out of one's eyes.

For years now whenever Christmas pageants are talked about in a certain little town in the Midwest, someone is sure to mention the name of Wallace
Purling. Wally's performance in one annual production of the Nativity play
has slipped into the realm of legend. But the old-timers who were in the
audience that night never tire of recalling exactly what happened.

Wally was nine that year and in the second grade, though he should have
been in the fourth. Most people in town knew that he had difficulty in keeping up. He was big and clumsy, slow in movement and mind. Still, Wally was
well liked by the other children in his town, all of whom were smaller than
he, though the boys had trouble hiding their irritation when the uncoordi-
nated Wally would ask to play ball with them.

Most often, they'd find a way to keep him off the field, but Wally would
hang around anyway—not sulking, just hoping. He was always a helpful boy, a
willing and smiling one, and the natural protector, paradoxically, of the
underdog. Sometimes if the older boys chased the younger ones away, it
would always be Wally who'd say, "Can't they stay? They're no bother."

Wally fancied the idea of being a shepherd with a flute in the Christmas pageant that year, but the play's director, Miss Lumbard, assigned him to a more
important role. After all, she reasoned, the innkeeper did not have too many
lines, and Wally's size would make his refusal of lodging to Joseph more forceful.

And so it happened that the usual large, partisan audience gathered for
the town's yuletide extravaganza of the crooks and creches, of bears, crowns,
halos, and a whole stageful of squeaky voices. No one on stage or off was
more caught up in the magic of the night than Wallace Purling. They said
later that he stood in the wings and watched the performance with such fas-

cination that from time to time Miss Lumbard had to make sure he didn't wander onstage before his cue.

Then the time came when Joseph appeared, slowly, tenderly guiding Mary to the door of the inn. Joseph knocked hard on the wooden door set into the painted backdrop. Wally the innkeeper was there, waiting.

"What do you want?" Wally said, swinging the door open with a brusque gesture.

"We seek lodging."

"Seek it elsewhere." Wally looked straight ahead but spoke vigorously. "The inn is filled."

"Sir, we have asked everywhere in vain. We have traveled far and are very weary."

"There is no room in this inn for you." Wally looked properly stern.

"Please, good innkeeper, this is my wife, Mary. She is heavy with child and needs a place to rest. Surely you must have some small corner for her. She is so tired."

Now for the first time, the innkeeper relaxed his stiff stance and looked down at Mary. With that, there was a long pause, long enough to make the audience a bit tense with embarrassment.

"No! Begone!" the prompter whispered from the wings.

"No! Wally repeated automatically. "Begone!"

Joseph sadly placed his arm around Mary, and Mary laid her head upon her husband's shoulder and the two of them started to move away. The innkeeper did not return inside his inn, however. Wally stood there in the doorway, watching the forlorn couple. His mouth was open, his brow creased with concern, his eyes filling unmistakably with tears.

And suddenly this Christmas pageant became different from all others.

"Don't go, Joseph," Wally called out. "Bring Mary back." And Wallace Purling's face grew into a bright smile. "You can have my room."

Some people in town thought that the pageant had been ruined. Yet there were others—many, many others—who considered it the most Christmas of all Christmas pageants they had ever seen.[1]

God Came Near

Max Lucado

We must be careful lest we romanticize the birth of Christ beyond reality. Nativity scenes have a way of making Jesus's birth unreasonably fairy-tale-like. What Jesus really endured in becoming a human being was to enter this world of harsh reality. Here in the midst of an inhuman humanity, he navigated existence to show us all the way.

She looks into the face of the baby. Her son. Her Lord. His Majesty. At this point in history, the human being who best understands who God is and what he is doing is a teenage girl in a smelly stable. She can't take her eyes off him. Somehow Mary knows she is holding God. *So this is he.* She remembers the words of the angel. "His kingdom will never end."

He looks like anything but a king. His face is prunish and red. His cry, though strong and healthy, is still the helpless and piercing cry of a baby. And he is absolutely dependent upon Mary for his well-being.

Majesty in the midst of the mundane. Holiness in the filth of sheep manure and sweat. Divinity entering the world on the floor of a stable, through the womb of a teenager and in the presence of a carpenter.[2]

Family Moment

There is something majestic about the birth of Jesus. But there is also something safe about it, as well. If we can keep Jesus a baby in our hearts and minds, helpless and small, we can control him so his majesty doesn't guide our life.

Jesus does not want to remain a baby in your life. He's a grown-up God, who delights in being the type of God whom you trust to follow every day. To do this means giving him the freedom to be Lord, not simply Savior.

Discuss what having Jesus as Lord means in a practical way to each individual's life. Giving up control is not an easy thing, no matter how much you love the Christmas story.

An Advent Prayer

Father in heaven, we are now about two weeks away from celebrating your Son's birth. As the days get closer and the holiday rush comes upon us, help us to keep in sight the true reason for the season. We love the presents, but we thank you for the present of your Son. We love the lights all around us, but we are grateful for the Light of the world. We love the decorations, but we are mindful that we don't have to decorate our life before we come to you; that you are more concerned with the internal decoration of having Jesus as Lord in our hearts. The days are getting closer, so we pause again to recognize you, our grown-up Lord and Savior. Help us always to have room for you in our hearts. In your name, amen.

Christmas is not a day or a season, but a condition of heart and mind. If we love our neighbors as ourselves; if in our riches we are poor in spirit and in our poverty we are rich in grace; if our love of others isn't for show, but suffers long and is kind; if when our brother asks for a loaf we give ourselves instead; if each day dawns in opportunity and sets in achievement, however small; then every day is Christ's day and Christmas is always near.[3]

—JAMES WALLINGFORD

No Room

Kathryn Slasor

"No room for Him," the keeper said
That night so long ago,
"My inn is crowded, don't you see,
The rooms now overflow."
"It's just a Child," he must have thought,
"A family, poor and plain;
My inn is filled with paying guests.
How could I dare explain?"

And thus, he turned aside from One
Who chose a humble birth
To enter into human form
And save all men on earth.
But lo, the shepherds in the hills
Were called, the Babe to greet;
They followed then the brilliant star
And worshipped at His feet!

"No room for Him," cry men today,
As through the world they plod;
"My life is crowded, don't you see?
I have no room for God.
How could I dare explain to all
My friends who question me,
That Jesus came to save my soul
From sin, to set me free?"

God, forbid that we become
As keepers of the inn,
And have our lives so crowded
That we have no room for Him.
But now, may we, Thy children dear,
Unworthy though we are,
Become as shepherds long ago,
And follow now His star!4

December 10

Today's Scripture:

Matthew 2:11

*They came to the house where the child was and saw
him with his mother, Mary, and they bowed down and
worshiped him. They opened their gifts and gave him
treasures of gold, frankincense, and myrrh.*

Suggested Longer Reading:

Matthew 2:1–15

The Magi's Visit

Gene Edwards

Many have speculated through the centuries about who the three wise men—the magi—might have been. Somewhere in the middle ages, a writer gave them names. Ever since, many others have used these names as they've retold the story of the eventful visit to the "small child," Jesus. It adds the human element needed by us to understand events so wonderful. In this short retelling by Gene Edwards, followed by a reading from Jim Bishop's classic book, The Day Christ Was Born, *try to put yourself in the middle of the action as Joseph and Mary are thrust into making decisions they surely thought they'd never have to make.*

The young couple accompanied the three magi to the barn where they had earlier stabled their camels.

"You are sure it is all right if we keep the gold and the myrrh and the frankincense?" asked Mary incredulously.

"They are small gifts for so great a king," assured Caspin.

"Well, you could stay the night," said Joseph. "There is an inn here in our village. And it is not crowded. In fact," he added with a grin, "I do not recall its being filled for over a year now."

"No," replied Gazerim as he mounted his camel. "We must return to Jerusalem with this great news. There are those waiting to hear."

"What do you mean?" asked Mary.

"We have promised to report back to the wise men of your religion, the ones who told us of the prophecy that the great king would be born here in this village."

"And more," said Akard, "yesterday it was our privilege to meet your present king. He was very pleased to know that there might be one born to equal greatness to himself. He asked us to return to him and tell him if we found the child who was born under David's star."

Joseph looked up into the face of Akard, "You met Herod the Great? He knows of the birth of our son?"

"Yes," said Akard. "We met him in his own palace. He was quite warm and hospitable. And he was very excited about the news."

Mary's face grew ashen. Joseph spoke, his words direct and strong.

"Before you return to speak to the king and to our leaders, would you first ask our God for wisdom? It may be that our Lord would have the birth of this child be kept secret for a while longer."

The three men exchanged glances and then nodded in assent. Before mounting his camel, Caspin walked over to Mary and planted a kiss on the forehead of the young boy she held in her arms. He then added a blessing in his heathen tongue.

As they rode off, Joseph wondered out loud, *What does this mean?* Mary crossed her arms as if to ward off a sudden chill. "Can it mean. . . ." The sentence remained unfinished.

Joseph completed the sentence, saying what they both were thinking: ". . . that the gentiles will come to worship Him just as much as may His own people?"

Joseph put his arm around Mary and led her into the house. Long into the night the young couple shared their thoughts about what they might do; but unable to come to any conclusion, they at last fell asleep. A few moments later, the door from the other realm opened into the small living room where the young couple and their child lay sleeping.

Gabriel knelt beside Joseph and stared into the young carpenter's face. Joseph turned restlessly. Gabriel did not move. Rather, he continued his motionless vigil. At last the archangel touched Joseph's forehead. Then, standing, he stepped back through the door.

Joseph woke with a start.

"Mary!" he cried. "A dream. I have had another dream! We must leave here immediately. It is some dreadful thing. Some monstrous evil. Herod will seek the life of our child. I know the dream is true. It was that same angel who appeared to me before. I saw him!"

Joseph sat up and turned toward Mary. "You are not going to like this, but I dare not disobey. The angel told me that we must take the baby out of Judea."

"Oh, Joseph, another move? Please, Joseph, not Nazareth."

"Mary, I told you, you are not going to like this. We are to go into Egypt."

"Egypt!" cried Mary. "Never! They worship bugs in Egypt!"

"Mary, we are not going to disobey the very angel who appeared to you, and who also has this odd habit of haunting *my* sleep. We are going to Egypt. We must. In the dream I heard the wail of thousands of mothers. I felt the death of little children all over our land."

Mary sat up, "The gold. This is why God sent us the gold. I knew we were not supposed to be rich. We are to use the gold to flee into Egypt."

Mary threw off the covers, speaking in an unbroken stream of words as she did. "We must leave immediately. Tonight. Joseph, wake that friend of yours, the owner of the stable. You know, Azzan. Buy a camel. We will use the camel for carrying our belongings and food and water. And buy a new donkey. A young, strong donkey. That floppy-eared, old donkey of yours will never make it to Egypt."

That night the young couple bought a camel they laughingly named Pharaoh, and the largest, strongest donkey they had ever seen, named Bashan. At dawn Joseph and Mary took Jesus and began their flight across the Sinai desert and into the land where men did, indeed, worship bugs.

It would be of Egypt that the young child, Jesus, would have His earliest memories. Nor would He forget that among the first things He ever learned was that He was a fugitive and a wayfarer upon this earthen ball.[1]

The Day Christ Was Born

JIM BISHOP

When the baby slept, and Mary and Joseph had time to discuss, in whispers, the wondrous things which had happened, and which would come in the future, they were beset by anxiety and they did not know what was expected of them. Joseph seemed at times to have a deeper appreciation of the destiny of the youngster. Mary, on the other hand, had an appreciation of each of the wonders of the birth of the Messiah, but seemed unable to group them into one big mural.

It was better this way because, had the Father permitted her to see the enormity of the whole plan, she would have been overwhelmed in the presence of Jesus and could not have discharged the duties of a good mother in the normal course of raising a child. Another factor was that the Son of God had come to earth to be born, to "grow in wisdom and in favor with God and men," to engage in a public ministry to show the true and only way to heaven, and to die in self-willed pain for all men. These things would not have been truly of earth if Jesus had not elected to be as human as his neighbors.

Neither Mary nor Joseph ever lost sight of the real mission of Jesus, nor of his divinity. They knew. In the years ahead there would be many strange and awesome things to remind them, again and again, that the human aspect was a lowering of God to man, whom he created and loved. The divine side would be hidden for more than thirty years and, when it was revealed publicly, it would be done at a marriage feast, and solely to please his mother. The sorrows were still far away.[2]

Family Moment

In God's own wisdom, he did not give Joseph and Mary the whole picture of their life together as parents of Jesus, or of the road their son would have to travel. If they had known the future, their hearts could not have borne the joy . . . or the grief. Any human parent would have been honored to have their child be the Savior of all men, but most would not have agreed to the method God chose to rid our hearts of the penalty of sin.

Today's question is brief: would you rather know the details of what your future holds or take one day at a time, live by faith in a God worthy of trust, and wake up each day saying, "Whatever, Lord. I am yours"?

Naturally, we don't really have the choice to see the future, but it's good to know where family members are in their ability to trust God for each step of their lives.

An Advent Prayer

Loving Father, help us remember the birth of Jesus, that we may share in the song of the angels, the gladness of the shepherds, and the worship of the wise men.

Close the door of hate and open the door of love all over the world.

Let kindness come with every gift and good desires with every greeting.

Deliver us from evil by the blessing which Christ brings, and teach us to be merry with clear hearts.

May the Christmas morning make us happy to be Your children, and the Christmas evening bring us to our beds with grateful thoughts, forgiving and forgiven, for Jesus's sake. Amen!

—ROBERT LOUIS STEVENSON

December 11

Matthew 6:25–26

*So I tell you, don't worry about the food or drink you need
to live, or about the clothes you need for your body. Life is
more than food, and the body is more than clothes. Look
at the birds in the air. They don't plant or harvest or store
food in barns, but your heavenly Father feeds them. And
you know that you are worth much more than the birds.*

Suggested Longer Readings:

Matthew 6:25–27 *and* **Proverbs 28:1**

Fear of Darkness

JIM BISHOP

Throughout the engagement, Mary, of course, lived with her parents and accepted the daily chores set out for her. At a time midway between engagement and formal marriage, Mary was alone one day and was visited by the angel Gabriel. She was alarmed, to be sure, but not as frightened as she would have been had she not heard stories of such visits from the elders. Mary lived after the days of the great prophets, the great visions, the visitations.

Gabriel stood before her and saw a dark, modest child of fourteen. "Rejoice, child of grace," he said. "The Lord is your helper. You are blessed beyond all women." Mary did not like the sound of the last sentence. Her hands began to shake. Why should she, a little country girl, be blessed beyond all women? Did it mean that she was about to die? Was she being taken, perhaps, to a far-off place, never again to see her mother and her father and—and—Joseph?

She said nothing. She tried to look away, not only because of terror but because it was considered bad manners in Judea for one to stare directly into the eyes of another, but her eyes were magnetized. She stared, and lowered her eyes, and stared again.

Gabriel's voice softened. "Do not tremble, Mary," he said. "You have found favor in the eyes of God. Behold: you are to be a mother and to bear a son, and to call him Jesus. He will be great: 'Son of the Most High' will be his title, and the Lord God will give to him the throne of his father, David. He will be king over the house of Jacob forever, and to his kingship there will be no end."

The words did not calm Mary. Vaguely, she understood that she was to be the mother of a king of kings, but who might this be and how could it occur when she was not even married?

"How will this be," she said shyly, "since I remain a virgin?"

It was Gabriel's turn to become specific. He stood in soft radiance in the room and explained. "The Holy Spirit will come upon you, and the power of the Most High will overshadow you. For this reason the child to be born will be acclaimed 'Holy' and 'Son of God.'" She now understood the words, but they added to her bewilderment. What the angel was saying, she reasoned, was something for which the Jews had been waiting for centuries: a Messiah, a Savior, God come to earth as he had promised long ago. Mary shook her head.

Not to her. Not to her.

Gabriel sensed that the child needed more proof. "Note, moreover," he said, "your relative Elizabeth, in her old age, has also conceived a son and is now in her sixth month—she who was called 'The barren.' Nothing indeed is impossible for God."

Her eyes lowered to the earthen floor, and her head inclined too. She comprehended. She also understood that the angel had told her about her old cousin Elizabeth, whom she had not seen in some time, so that the fruitfulness of her kinswoman would be the earthly seal of proof to the heavenly words. She, a young virgin, was to be blessed by the Holy Spirit, and she would bear a male child who would be God. It was an enormous honor, but she had been taught to accept and obey the will of God from the first moments of early understanding.

"Regard me as the humble servant of the Lord," she murmured. "May all that you have said be fulfilled in me."

The angel stood before her in silence, fading slowly from her vision, bit by bit, until all that was visible was the wall.[1]

Family Moment

Have you ever thought that there are *good* things that could spark fear? The best thing in the world was happening to Mary, yet fear and trembling was her first reaction. Natural? Yes, very! Do you think Mary would have initially thought being pregnant and not married, but pregnant with God's Son, would be a good thing? When do you think she made that transition from fear to faith? Why at this time?

Take a few moments to talk about potential good things that can happen in each family member's life that may take some time to get used to. Examples could be: sharing your faith in a small group of friends; a trial of some sort that causes you to depend on God beyond what you thought capable (can you name a few?); or losing a job so you have to move out of the nest to pursue a dream.

What is the key to responding to situations in faith, not fear?

An Advent Prayer

Lord of all creation, we're mindful that in this life you have promised trials, but you've also promised not to leave us in the dark to endure these trials alone. Help us to look at each circumstance that comes our way through the eyes of faith, not fear. Help us to respond with optimism about what we can learn and how we can grow, instead of annoyance that our life has been interrupted. Lord, you are the center of our lives, so as the storm rages around us, help us to keep you in the eye of the storm so that we might not fear. In your name, amen.

Faith is the trying of the things unseen— the putting of them to the test; and whatever your doubts and fears are, try God by obedience, and then you will get help to carry you on. Less than that will not do.

—GEORGE MACDONALD

December 12

Today's Scripture:

Micah 5:3

The Lord will give up his people until the one who is having a baby gives birth; then the rest of his relatives will return to the people of Israel.

Suggested Longer Reading:

Micah 5:2–5

The Little Match Girl

Hans Christian Andersen

It was terribly cold; it snowed and was already almost dark, and evening came on, the last evening of the year. In the cold and gloom a poor little girl, bareheaded and barefoot, was walking through the streets. When she left her own house she certainly had had slippers on, but of what use were they? They were very big slippers, and her mother had used them till then, so big were they. The little maid lost them as she slipped across the road, where two carriages were rattling by terribly fast. One slipper was not to be found again, and a boy had seized the other and run away with it.

He thought he could use it very well as a cradle someday when he had children of his own. So now the little girl went on with her little naked feet, which were quite red and blue with the cold. In an old apron she carried a number of matches, and a bundle of them in her hand. No one had bought anything from her all day, and no one had given her a farthing.

Shivering with cold and hunger, she crept along, a picture of misery, poor little girl! The snowflakes covered her long fair hair, which fell in pretty curls over her neck; but she did not think of that now. In all the windows lights were shining, and there was a glorious smell of roast goose, for it was New Year's Eve. Yes, she thought of that!

In a corner formed by two houses, one of which projected beyond the other, she sat down, cowering. She had drawn up her little feet, but she was still colder, and she did not dare to go home, for she had sold no matches and did not bring a farthing of money. From her father she would certainly receive a beating; and besides, it was cold at home, for they had nothing over them but a roof through which the wind whistled, though the largest rents had been stopped with straw and rags.

Her little hands were almost benumbed with the cold. Ah, a match might do her good, if she could only draw one from the bundle and rub it against the wall and warm her hands at it. She drew one out. R-r-atch! How it sputtered and burned! It was a warm, bright flame, like a little candle, when she held her hands over it; it was a wonderful little light! It really seemed to the little girl as if she sat before a great polished stove with bright brass feet and a brass cover. How the fire burned! How comfortable it was! But the little flame went out, the stove vanished, and she had only the remains of the burnt match in her hand.

A second was rubbed against the wall. It burned up, and when the light fell upon the wall it became transparent like a thin veil, and she could see through it into the room. On the table a snow-white cloth was spread; upon it stood a shining dinner service; the roast goose smoked gloriously, stuffed with apples and dried plums. And, what was still more splendid to behold, the goose hopped down from the dish and waddled along the floor, with a knife and fork in its breast, to the little girl. Then the match went out and only the thick, damp, cold wall was before her. She lighted another match. Then she was sitting under a beautiful Christmas tree; it was greater and more ornamented than the one she had seen through the glass door at the rich merchant's. Thousands of candles burned upon the green branches, and colored pictures like those in the print shop looked down upon them. The little girl stretched forth her hand toward them, then the match went out. The Christmas lights mounted higher. She saw them now as stars in the sky; one of them fell down, forming a long line of fire.

"Now someone is dying," thought the little girl, for her old grandmother, the only person who had loved her, and who was now dead, had told her that when a star fell down a soul mounted up to God.

She rubbed another match against the wall; it became bright again, and in the brightness the old grandmother stood clear and shining, mild and lovely.

"Grandmother!" cried the child. "Oh, take me with you! I know you will go when the match is burned out. You will vanish like the warm fire, the warm food, and the great, glorious Christmas tree!"

And she hastily rubbed the whole bundle of matches, for she wished to hold her grandmother fast. And the matches burned with such a glow that it became brighter than in the middle of the day; grandmother had never been so large or so beautiful. She took the little girl in her arms, and both flew in brightness and joy above the earth, very, very high, and up there was neither cold, nor hunger, nor care—they were with God.

But in the corner, leaning against the wall, sat the poor girl with red cheeks and smiling mouth, frozen to death on the last evening of the old year. The New Year's sun rose upon a little corpse! The child sat there, stiff and cold, with the matches, of which one bundle was burned. "She wanted to warm herself," the people said. No one imagined what a beautiful thing she had seen and in what glory she had gone with her grandmother to the New Year's Day.[1]

Family Moment

Do a checkup on how the family is doing midway through Advent to Christmas. Ask everyone if they think they are missing anything they shouldn't. "Are we fulfilling our goal of placing Christ right in the center of our Christmas celebration? What more could we be doing?"

An Advent Prayer

Father, we're just a few days away from celebrating your birth and your life here on earth. We don't want to miss anything as we do this, so help us continue to focus on you and not on all of our outward displays of celebration. We want to love you deeper, appreciate you more, stay thankful for all we have, but most of all simply rejoice that we have breath to sing your praise and lips to speak your love to all who will listen. In your Son's name, amen.

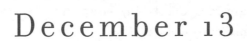

December 13

Ezekiel 34:11

This is what the Lord God says: I, myself, will search for my sheep and take care of them.

Suggested Longer Reading:

Ezekiel 34:11–16

A Shepherd

HEYWOOD BROUN

The host of heaven and the angel of the Lord had filled the sky with radiance. Now the glory of God was gone and the shepherds and the sheep stood under dim starlight. The men were shaken by the wonders they had seen and heard and, like the animals, they huddled close.

"Let us now," said the eldest of the shepherds, "go even unto Bethlehem and see this thing which has come to pass, which the Lord hath made known unto us."

The City of David lay beyond a far, high hill, upon the crest of which there danced a star. The men made haste to be away, but as they broke out of the circle there was one called Amos who remained. He dug his crook into the turf and clung to it.

"Come," cried the eldest of the shepherds, but Amos shook his head. They marveled, and one called out, "It is true. It was an angel. You heard the tidings. A Savior is born!"

"I heard," said Amos. "I will abide."

The eldest walked back from the road to the little knoll on which Amos stood.

"You do not understand," the old man told him. "We have a sign from God. An angel commanded us. We go to worship the Savior, who is even now born in Bethlehem. God has made His will manifest."

"It is not in my heart," replied Amos.

And now the eldest of the shepherds was angry.

"With your own eyes," he cried out, "you have seen the host of heaven in these dark hills. And you heard, for it was like thunder when 'Glory to God in the highest' came ringing to us out of the night."

And again Amos said, "It is not in my heart."

Another shepherd then broke in. "Because the hills stand and the sky has not fallen, it is not enough for Amos. He must have something louder than the voice of God."

Amos held more tightly to his crook and answered, "I have need of a whisper."

They laughed at him and said, "What should this voice say in your ear?"

He was silent and they pressed about him and shouted mockingly, "Tell us now. What says the God of Amos, the little shepherd of a hundred sheep?"

Meekness fell away from him. He took his hands from off the crook and raised them high.

"I too am a god," said Amos in a loud, strange voice, "and to my hundred sheep I am a savior."

And when the din of the angry shepherds about him slackened, Amos pointed to his hundred.

"See my flock," he said. "See the fright of them. The fear of the bright angel and of the voices is still upon them. God is busy in Bethlehem. He has no time for a hundred sheep. They are my sheep. I will abide."

This the others did not take so much amiss, for they saw that there was a terror in all the flocks and they too knew the ways of sheep. And before the shepherds departed on the road to Bethlehem toward the bright star, each talked to Amos and told him what he should do for the care of the several flocks. And yet one or two turned back a moment to taunt Amos, before they reached the dip in the road which led to the City of David. It was said, "We shall see new glories at the throne of God, and you, Amos, you will see sheep."

Amos paid no heed, for he thought to himself, "One shepherd the less will not matter at the throne of God." Nor did he have time to be troubled that he was not to see the Child who was come to save the world. There was much to be done among the flocks and Amos walked between the sheep and made under his tongue a clucking noise, which was a way he had, and to his hundred and to the others it was a sound more fine and friendly than the voice of the bright angel. Presently the animals ceased to tremble and they began to graze as the sun came up over the hill where the star had been.

"For sheep," said Amos to himself, "the angels shine too much. A shepherd is better."

With the morning the others came up the road from Bethlehem, and they told Amos of the manger and of the wise men who had mingled there with shepherds. And they described to him the gifts: gold, frankincense and myrrh. And when they were done they said, "And did you see wonders here in the fields with the sheep?"

Amos told them, "Now my hundred are one hundred and one," and he showed them a lamb which had been born just before the dawn.

"Was there for this a great voice out of heaven?" asked the eldest of the shepherds.

Amos shook his head and smiled, and there was upon his face that which seemed to the shepherds a wonder even in a night of wonders.

"To my heart," he said, "there came a whisper."[1]

Family Moment

The image of Jesus as our Shepherd is perfect. We often wander around like dumb sheep, looking for someone else to lead us to greener pastures. All the while we rely on his protection from the wolves out there who seek to destroy everything. But no matter how much we rely on the Good Shepherd's protection, the wolves still come.

As a family, discuss the things in the world that fight against the closeness a family can have. "What are the influences that pull us away from each other?" Each family member ought to notice something different, since you go to different places each day.

How can the family do an even better job of protecting each other from influences that seek to pull us apart?

An Advent Prayer

Precious Father and Shepherd, even now, you're looking over us, protecting us from all of the influences that seek to tear us apart. We're very thankful that you have the power and wisdom to do this not just for us but for all of the families who call upon your name. We are grateful that you're a big God fully able to protect us, but we pray that we're not just dumb sheep in your eyes. Give us the wisdom and discernment we need to identify and battle against those forces who would seek to tear us apart. We're relying on you, Good Shepherd, to guide our souls safely to you. Amen.

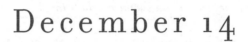

December 14

Today's Scripture:

Luke 2:15–16

When the angels left them and went back to heaven, the shepherds said to each other, "Let's go to Bethlehem. Let's see this thing that has happened which the Lord has told us about." So the shepherds went quickly and found Mary and Joseph and the baby, who was lying in a feeding box.

Suggested Longer Reading:

Luke 2:15–20

The Unexpected Christmas

MARGUERITE NIXON

> What can one do when a torrential storm closes off the road and one is
> forced to spend Christmas Eve with strangers . . . strangers who have so very
> little . . . just a poor farm . . . and some animals in a barn?

We were well over halfway to our farm in East Texas when the storm broke. Lightning flashed, thunder crashed, and a tree fell with a great ripping noise. When the rain poured in such a flood that we could not see the road, my husband drove off onto what seemed to be a bit of clearing deep in the piney woods.

As we waited I sensed we would not get to the farm that night to celebrate Christmas Eve with our family. We were sitting there, miserable and dejected, when I heard a knocking on my window. A man with a lantern stood there, beckoning us to follow him. My husband and I splashed after him up the path to his house.

A woman with a lamp in her hand stood in the doorway of an old house; a boy of about twelve, and a little girl stood beside her. We went in, soaked and dripping, and the family moved aside in order that we might have the warmth of the fire. With the volubility of city people, my husband and I began to talk, explaining our plans. And with the quietness of people who live in the silence of the woods, they listened.

"The bridge on Caney Creek is out. You are welcome to spend the night with us," the man said. And though we told them we thought it was an imposition, especially on Christmas Eve, they insisted. After we had visited a while longer, the man got up and took the Bible from the mantel. "It's our custom to read the story from Saint Luke on Christmas Eve," he said, and without another word he began.

"'And she brought forth her firstborn Son, and wrapped Him in swaddling clothes, and laid Him in a manger.'"

The children sat up eagerly, their eyes bright in anticipation, while their father read on.

"'And there were in the same country shepherds abiding in the field, keeping watch over their flocks by night.'"

I looked at his strong face. He could have been one of them. When he finished reading and closed the Bible, the little children knelt by their chairs. The mother and father were kneeling and, without any conscious will of my own, I found myself joining them. Then I saw my husband, without any embarrassment at all, kneel also.

When we arose, I looked around the room. There were no brightly-wrapped packages or cards, only a small, unadorned holly tree on the mantel. Yet the spirit of Christmas was never more real to me.

The little boy broke the silence. "We always feed the cattle at 12:00 on Christmas Eve. Come with us."

The barn was warm and fragrant with the smell of hay and dried corn. A cow and a horse greeted us, and there was a goat with a tiny, woolly kid that came up to be petted. *This is like the stable where the Baby was born*, I thought. *Here is the manger, and the gentle animals to keep watch.*

When we returned to the house, there was an air of festivity and the serving of juice and fruitcake. Later, we bedded down on a mattress made of corn shucks. As I turned into a comfortable position, they rustled under me and sent up a faint fragrance exactly like that in the barn. My heart said, *You are sleeping in the stable like the Christ Child did.* As I drifted into a profound sleep, I knew that the light coming through the old pine shutters was the Star shining on that quiet house.

The family all walked down the path to the car with us the next morning. I was so filled with the Spirit of Christmas they had given me that I could find no words. Suddenly I thought of the gifts in the back seat of our car for our family.

I began to hand them out. My husband's gray woolen socks went to the man. The red sweater I had bought for my sister went to the mother. I gave away two boxes of candy, the white mittens, and the leather gloves while my husband nodded approval.

And when I was breathless from reaching in and out of the car and the family stood there loaded with the gaiety of Christmas packages, the mother spoke for all of them. "We thank you," she said simply. And then she said, "Wait."

She hurried up the path to the house and came back with a quilt folded across her arms. It was beautifully handmade; the pattern was the Star of Bethlehem. I looked up at the tall beautiful pines because my throat hurt and I could not speak. It was indeed Christmas.

Every Christmas Eve since then I sleep under that quilt, the Star of Bethlehem, and in memory I visit the stable and smell again the corn shucks, and the meaning of Christmas abides with me once more.[1]

Family Moment

If you are willing to try to celebrate Christmas as Mary and the shepherds did, don't begin with verse 17, which tells us to tell others about Jesus. Begin with verses 18-20, which tell us to wonder at the birth of Jesus, to ponder its meaning, and to praise God for it. Praise God for sending Jesus. Think about why Jesus came to earth on that cold night so long ago. And marvel that, because of his birth, life, death, and resurrection, you have not suffered God's just punishment for your sins but rather have been saved from them.

When you have really thought about these things and thanked God for them, go back to verse 17 and tell others, as the shepherds did. And last, think about what you can give back to the Lord for this amazing gift.

An Advent Prayer

Dear Lord, who lives in our hearts. First, we want to rediscover the wonder of what it means to be a Christian who can celebrate all that you have done. It's more wonderful than we know, but this Advent season, we pray you will show us more wonder. We want this, Lord. Second, Father, we want to, in some way, be like the shepherds who had to tell others what they saw. Help us to be grateful for our salvation. To be like a beggar who seeks to tell another beggar where to find bread. You've led us to the Bread of Life, even Jesus, so show us how we can give this bread away to all who have a hunger in their souls for something more. In Jesus's name. Amen.

First, behold how very ordinary and common things are to us that transpire on earth, and yet how high they are regarded in heaven. On earth it occurs in this wise: Here is a poor young woman, Mary of Nazareth, not highly esteemed, but of the humblest citizens of the village. No one is conscious of the great wonder she bears, she is silent, keeps her own counsel, and regards herself as the lowliest in the town. She starts out with her husband Joseph; very likely they had no servant, and he had to do the work of master and servant, and she that of mistress and maid. They were therefore obliged to leave their home unoccupied, or commend it to the care of others.

—MARTIN LUTHER

December 15

Ephesians 4:32

*Be kind and loving to each other, and forgive each other
just as God forgave you in Christ.*

Suggested Longer Reading:

Colossians 3:16–17

The Fir Tree

HANS CHRISTIAN ANDERSEN

Hans Christian Andersen was a Dutch writer in the nineteenth century who penned many stories like the one below. His most famous was The Ugly Duckling. *While the reality of this particular story is questioned even by the author, the truth revealed by the tale cannot be questioned. See if you agree.*

In a small cottage on the borders of a forest lived a poor laborer, who gained a scanty living by cutting wood. He had a wife and two children who helped him in his work. The boy's name was Valentine, and the girl was called Mary. They were obedient, good children, and a great comfort to their parents.

One winter evening, this happy little family was sitting quietly round the hearth, the snow and the wind raging outside, while they ate their supper of dry bread, when a gentle tap was heard on the window, and a childish voice cried from outside, "Oh, let me in, I pray! I am a poor child, with nothing to eat, and no home to go to, and I shall die of cold and hunger unless you let me in." Valentine and Mary jumped up from the table and ran to open the door, saying, "Come in, poor little child! We have not much to give you, but whatever we have we will share with you."

The stranger-child came in and warmed his frozen hands and feet at the fire, and the children gave him the best they had to eat, saying, "You must be tired, too, poor child! Lie down on our bed; we can sleep on the bench for one night."

Then said the little stranger-child, "Thank God for all your kindness to me." So they took their little guest into their sleeping-place, laid him on the bed, covered him over, and said to each other, "How thankful we ought to be! We have warm rooms and a cozy bed, while this poor child has only heaven for his roof and the cold earth for his sleeping-place."

When the father and mother went to bed, Mary and Valentine lay quite contentedly on the bench near the fire, saying, before they fell asleep, "The stranger-child will be happy tonight in his warm bed."

These kind children had not slept many hours before Mary awoke, and softly whispered to her brother, "Valentine, dear brother, wake, and listen to the sweet music under the window."

Then Valentine rubbed his eyes and listened. It was sweet music indeed, and sounded like beautiful voices singing to the tones of a harp:

> *Oh holy Child, we greet thee! Bringing*
> *Sweet strains of harp to aid our singing.*
> *Thou holy Child, in peace art sleeping,*
> *While we our watch without are keeping.*
> *Blest be the house wherein thou liest,*
> *Happiest on earth, to heaven the nighest.*

The children listened, while a solemn joy filled their hearts, then they stepped softly to the window to see who was singing.

In the east was a streak of rosy dawn, and in its light they saw a group of children standing in front of the house, clothed in sparkling garments and holding golden harps. Amazed at the sight, the brother and sister were still gazing out the window when they heard a sound behind them. Turning they discovered the stranger-child standing before them. "I am the little Christ child," he said. "I wander through the world bringing peace and happiness to children. You took me in and cared for me when you thought I was a poor child, and now you shall have my blessing for what you have done."

A fir tree grew near the little house; and from this the Christ-child broke a twig and planted it in the ground. He looked directly at Valentine and Mary and said, "This twig shall become a tree, and shall bring forth fruit year by year for you."

No sooner had he done this than he vanished, and with him the choir of angels. The fir-branch grew and became a Christmas tree, and on its branches hung golden apples and silver nuts every Christmas.

Such is the story told to German children concerning their beautiful Christmas trees, though we know that this is only a fable. The real Christ-child can never be wandering cold and homeless in our world, because he is safe in heaven by his Father's side; yet we may gather from this story the same truth which the Bible plainly tells us—that to anyone who helps another person, it will be counted to them as if he had done it to Christ himself. "In as much as ye have done it unto the least of these my brethren, ye have done it unto me."[1]

Family Moment

Kindness. When you think of that word, what picture comes to mind? Who or what do you think of? What have they done or said that has made you feel warm and that you mattered?

Every day, we have the chance to represent Jesus to anyone God brings our way. We can be kind in what we *do*, what we *say*, even in our *body language* (posture, eye contact) to others who may just want to see if their lives matter to other human souls.

Ask family members how they best express kindness.

Now, ask them how they can improve a little bit more in being kind to others.

An Advent Prayer

Dear kind Lord, thank you that kindness is part of your character from which we can learn. You were kind to everyone who needed kindness. You reached out to touch those who needed your touch; you said the right words to those who were hurting; you showed by every action in your life that people were more important than anything else on earth. Help us to learn from the examples you set for us, but help us to learn this lesson best. We want to be kind to others, for in doing so, we show we are being kind to you. In Jesus's name, amen.

Christmas Facts

Legend of the Christmas Tree

How did the Christmas tree come to play such an important part in the observance of Christmas?

There is a legend that comes down to us from the early days of Christianity in England. One of those helping to spread Christianity was a monk named Wilfred (later Saint Wilfred). One day, surrounded by a group of his converts, he struck down a huge oak tree, which, to them, was an object of worship.

As it fell to the earth, the oak tree split into four pieces, and from its center sprung up a young fir tree. The crowd gazed in amazement.

Wilfred let his axe drop and turned to speak. "This little tree shall be your Holy tree tonight. It is the wood of peace, for your houses are built of the fir. It is the sign of an endless life, for its leaves are evergreen. See how it points toward the heavens?

"Let this be called the tree of the Christ Child. Gather about it, not in the wilderness but in your homes. There it will be surrounded with loving gifts and rites of kindness."

And to this day, that is why the fir tree is one of our loveliest symbols of Christmas.

O Christmas Tree

Traditional German

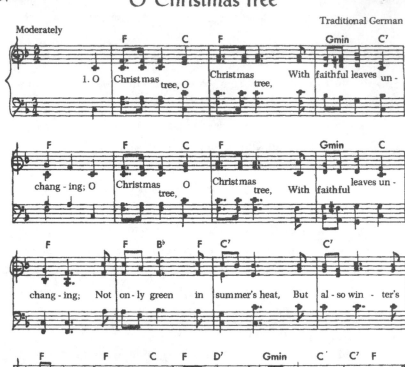

2.
O Christmas tree, O Christmas tree,
Of all the trees most lovely;
Each year you bring to me delight
Gleaming in the Christmas light.
O Christmas tree, O Christmas tree,
Of all the trees most lovely.

3.
O Christmas tree, O Christmas tree,
Your leaves will teach me, also,
That hope and love and faithfulness
Are precious things I can possess.
O Christmas tree, O Christmas tree,
Your leaves will teach me, also.

December 16

Today's Scripture:

Psalm 90:12

*Teach us how short our lives really are so that we may be
wise.*

Suggested Longer Reading:

Luke 24:13–35

My Most Memorable Christmas

Catherine Marshall

We spent Christmas 1960 at Evergreen Farm in Lincoln, Virginia—the home of my parents. With us were my sister and her husband—Emmy and Harlow Hoskins—and their two girls, Lynn and Winifred. It meant a typical family occasion with our three children, Linda, Chester, and Jeffrey, along with Peter John who was then a senior at Yale. Five children can make an old farmhouse ring with the yuletide spirit.

For our Christmas Eve service, Lynn and Linda had prepared an improvised altar before the living room fireplace. Jeffrey and Winifred (the youngest grandchildren) lighted all the candles. Then with all of his family gathered around him, my father read Luke's incomparable account of the first Christmas. There was carol singing, with Chester and Winifred singing a duet, "Hark, the Herald Angels Sing," in their high, piping voices. Then my mother, the storyteller of the family, gave us an old favorite, "Why the Chimes Rang." She made us see the ragged little boy creeping up that long cathedral aisle and slipping his gift onto the altar.

Then she said, "You know, I'd like to make a suggestion to the family. The floor underneath the tree in the den is piled high with gifts we're giving to one another. But we're celebrating Christ's birthday, not each other's. This is His time of year. What are we going to give to Jesus?"

The room began to hum with voices, comparing notes. But Mother went on, "Let's think about it for a few moments. Then we'll go around the circle and each of us will tell what gift he will lay on the altar for Christ's birthday."

Chester, age seven, crept close to his father for a whispered consultation. Then he said shyly, "What I'd like to give Jesus this year is not to lose my temper anymore."

Jeffrey, age four, who had been slow in night training, was delightfully specific. "I'll give Him my diapers."

Winifred said softly that she was going to give Jesus good grades in school. Lynn's was, "To be a better father, which means a gift of more patience."

And so it went . . . on around the group. Peter John's was short but significant. "What I want to give to Christ is a more dedicated life." I was to remember that statement five years later at the moment of his ordination into the Presbyterian ministry when he stood so straight and so tall and answered so resoundingly, "I do so believe. . . . I do so promise. . . ." Yet at Christmas time, 1960, the ministry was probably the last thing he expected to get into.

Then it was my father's turn. "I certainly don't want to inject too solemn a note into this," he said, "but somehow I know that this is the last Christmas I'll be sitting in this room with my family gathered around me like this."

We gasped and protested, but he would not be stopped. "No, I so much want to say this. I've had a most wonderful life. Long, long ago I gave my life to Christ. Though I've tried to serve Him, I've failed Him often. But He has blessed me with great riches—especially my family. I want to say this while you're all here. I may not have another chance. Even after I go on into the next life, I'll still be with you. And, of course, I'll be waiting for each one of you there."

There was love in his brown eyes—and tears in ours. No one said anything for a moment. Time seemed to stand still in the quiet room. Firelight and candlelight played on the children's faces as they looked at their grandfather, trying to grasp what he was saying. The fragrance of balsam and cedar was in the air. The old windowpanes reflected back the red glow of Christmas lights.

Father did leave this world four months later—on May first. His passing was like a benediction. It happened one afternoon as he sat quietly in a chair in the little village post office talking to some of his friends. His heart just stopped beating. That Christmas Eve he had known with a strange sureness that the time was close.

Every time I think of Father now, I can see that scene in the living room—like a jewel of a moment set in the ordinary moments that make up our days. For that brief time real values came clearly into focus: Father's gratitude for life; Mother's strong faith; my husband's quiet strength; my son's inner yearning momentarily shining through blurred youthful ambitions; the eager faces of children groping toward understanding and truth; the reality of the love of God as our thoughts focused on Him whose birth we were commemorating.

It was my most memorable Christmas.[1]

Family Moment

Think of all the memories we've had as a family during Christmas through the years. What memories do you count as the best? Why?

How could this family make our memories even sweeter than they already are?

An Advent Prayer

Father God, show us how precious each family member is this season. Teach us to number our days so that we might honor you and love others. Give us a new appreciation of how unique and beloved each of us is to the others. Amid the things that bother us the most, let us not lose sight that you have made this family what it is. Help us rest in your wonderful plan that we should go through life together for all of the days we have breath. We're grateful, and our hearts are filled with love for you and each other. Amen.

O Come, O Come, Emmanuel

Latin

Advent Carol
Plainsong

Moderately

1. O come, O come, Em - man — u - el, And
ran - som cap - tive Is — ra - el, That mourns in lone - ly
ex — ile here, Un - til the Son of God — ap -

Refrain

pear. Re - joice, re - joice, Em - man — u -
el, Shall come to Thee, O Is — ra - el.

Christmas is the day that holds all time together.

—ALEXANDER SMITH

December 17

Today's Scripture:

Psalm 24:1

The earth belongs to the Lord, and everything in it—the world and all its people.

Suggested Longer Reading:

Psalm 24:1–10

A String of Blue Beads

FULTON OURSLER

One of the loveliest of all Christmas short stories was penned by Fulton Oursler. Oursler's story reminds us that possessions without someone to share them with are hollow and meaningless. He also reminds us once again that one can't pay more than "all one has" for a gift.

Pete Richards was the loneliest man in town on the day Jean Grace opened his door. You may have seen something in the newspapers about the incident at the time it happened, although neither his name nor hers was published, nor was the full story told as I tell it here.

Pete's shop had come down to him from his grandfather. The little front window was strewn with a disarray of old-fashioned things: bracelets and lockets worn in days before the Civil War, gold rings and silver boxes, images of jade and ivory, porcelain figurines.

On this winter's afternoon a child was standing there, her forehead against the glass, earnest and enormous eyes studying each discarded treasure as if she were looking for something quite special. Finally she straightened up with a satisfied air and entered the store.

The shadowy interior of Pete Richards's establishment was even more cluttered than his show window. Shelves were stacked with jewel caskets, dueling pistols, clocks, and lamps, and the floor was heaped with andirons and mandolins and things hard to find a name for.

Behind the counter stood Pete himself, a man not more than thirty but with hair already turning gray. There was a bleak air about him as he looked at the small customer who flattened her ungloved hands on the counter.

"Mister," she began, "would you please let me look at that string of blue beads in the window?"

Pete parted the draperies and lifted out a necklace. The turquoise stones gleamed brightly against the pallor of his palm as he spread the ornament before her.

"They're just perfect," said the child, entirely to herself. "Will you wrap them up pretty for me, please?"

Pete studied her with a stony air. "Are you buying these for someone?"

"They're for my big sister. She takes care of me. You see, this will be the first Christmas since Mother died. I've been looking for the most wonderful Christmas present for my sister."

"How much money do you have?" asked Pete warily.

She had been busily untying the knots in a handkerchief and now she poured out a handful of pennies on the counter.

"I emptied my bank," she explained simply.

Pete Richards looked at her thoughtfully. Then he carefully drew back the necklace. The price tag was visible to him but not to her. How could he tell her? The trusting look of her blue eyes smote him like the pain of an old wound.

"Just a minute," he said, and turned toward the back of the store. Over his shoulder he called, "What's your name?" He was very busy about something.

"Jean Grace."

When Pete returned to where Jean Grace waited, a package lay in his hand, wrapped in scarlet paper and tied with a bow of green ribbon. "There you are," he said shortly. "Don't lose it on the way home."

She smiled happily at him over her shoulder as she ran out the door. Through the window he watched her go, while desolation flooded his thoughts. Something about Jean Grace and her string of beads had stirred him to the depths of a grief that would not stay buried. The child's hair was wheat yellow, her eyes sea blue, and once upon a time, not long before, Pete had been in love with a girl with hair of that same yellow and with eyes just as blue. And the turquoise necklace was to have been hers.

But there had come a rainy night—a truck skidding on a slippery road—and the life was crushed out of his dream.

Since then Pete Richards had lived too much with his grief in solitude. He was politely attentive to customers, but after business hours his world seemed irrevocably empty. He was trying to forget in a self-pitying haze that deepened day by day.

The blue eyes of Jean Grace jolted him into acute remembrance of what he had lost. The pain of it made him recoil from the exuberance of holiday shoppers. During the next ten days trade was brisk; chattering men swarmed in, fingering trinkets, trying to bargain. When the last customer had gone, late on Christmas Eve, he sighed with relief. It was over for another year. But for Pete Richards the night was not quite over.

The door opened and a young woman hurried in. With an inexplicable start, he realized that she looked familiar, yet he could not remember when or where he had seen her before. Her hair was golden yellow and her large eyes were blue. Without speaking, she drew from her purse a package loosely unwrapped in its red paper, a bow of green ribbon with it. Presently the string of blue beads lay gleaming again before him.

"Did this come from your shop?" she asked.

Pete raised his eyes to hers and answered softly, "Yes, it did."

"Are the stones real?"

"Yes. Not the finest quality—but real."

"Can you remember who it was you sold them to?"

"She was a small girl. Her name was Jean. She bought them for her older sister's Christmas present."

"How much are they worth?"

"The price," he told her solemnly, "is always a confidential matter between the seller and the customer."

"But Jean has never had more than a few pennies of spending money. How could she pay for them?"

Pete was folding the gay paper back into its creases, rewrapping the little package just as neatly as before.

"She paid the biggest price anyone can ever pay," he said. "She gave all she had."

There was a silence then that filled the little curio shop. He saw the far-away steeple, a bell began ringing. The sound of the distant chiming, the little package lying on the counter, the question in the eyes of the girl, and the strange feeling of renewal struggling unreasonably in the heart of the man, all had come to be because of the love of a child.

"But why did you do it?"

He held out the gift in his hand.

"It's already Christmas morning," he said. "And it's my misfortune that I have no one to give anything to. Will you let me see you home and wish you a Merry Christmas at your door?"

And so, to the sound of many bells and in the midst of happy people, Pete Richards and a girl whose name he had yet to hear, walked out into the beginning of the great day that brings hope into the world for us all.[1]

Family Moment

Ask family members if it is hard or easy for them to believe that all of the heroes of the Bible were actually human beings. How do you imagine them?

Do you think God is put off by our thinking or asking these questions about people in the Bible, even if we might never know the answers?

Do you think God understands our humanness, or does he expect us to have our heads in the clouds? Does God have *his* head in the clouds?

An Advent Prayer

Lord of heaven and earth, we thank you today that you understand completely our human nature. You understand our questions, no matter how funny or insignificant. And you understand our bigger questions about life too. Lord, you understand us! You made us, you placed us here on this earth, you gave us each other to love and care for, and you challenge us each day to think more deeply about you. Thank you that no question is out of bounds, that you aren't afraid of anything, and that you won't become angry with us for allowing our minds to wonder. Lord, help our wonder of life always turn to wonder of you. In Jesus's name, amen.

Frankincense and Myrrh and Gold

ETHEL DIETRICH

The tree is trimmed, the stockings hung,
The stories read, the carols sung,
I've placed the gifts beneath the tree
The stockings bulge with mystery.
The scene is set for Christmas Eve,
But then before I turn to leave
There in the stable small and brown
I lay the Baby Jesus down
Soft gently in his manger bed,
Wisps of straw to pillow his head.
"Welcome, welcome, Little One,
Child of Mary, God's own Son."

Somehow I feel the hours spent
In making Christmas evident—
The wrappings sparkling green and red,
The sugar cakes and gingerbread,
Beribboned wreaths and candleshine—
All these are proferred gifts of mine
Made up of thoughts and love and time,
Just simple gestures, not sublime,
But offered in His name today,
My efforts seem in some small way
Much like the Magi's gifts of old—
My frankincense and myrrh and gold.[2]

December 18

Today's Scripture:

Matthew 2:16

When Herod saw that the wise men had tricked him, he was furious. So he gave an order to kill all the baby boys in Bethlehem and in the surrounding area who were two years old or younger. This was in keeping with the time he learned from the wise men.

Suggested Longer Reading:

Matthew 2:16–23

The Letter

RETOLD FROM PUBLIC RECORDS

In the shabby basement of an old house in Atlanta, Georgia, lived a young widow and her little girl. During the Civil War, she had married a young Confederate soldier, against her Yankee father's will, and had moved with him south, to Atlanta. Her wealthy father, angry and hurt at what he considered to be her disloyalty, both to him and the North, told her never to come back.

The soldier had died bravely during the war, and his death left his wife and child without any support. Alone in Atlanta, Margaret did washing, ironing, and other menial jobs that she could find to help her scrape by and feed little Anna. Their clothes became ragged, and they were both ill from sleeping in the damp, cold basement.

Anna loved to hear her mother's stories about her home in the North. She sat in her mother's lap and listened for hours to descriptions of the big, brick house in Boston, the sprawling shade trees, the beautiful flower gardens, and the wide grassy lawn. She loved to imagine the horses trotting across the meadow, the smell of bread baking in the kitchen, and the soft feel of the four-poster feather beds. Although Anna had never seen her mother's home, she thought it must be marvelous and secretly hoped that someday they would go there to live.

Margaret often sat looking wistfully up through the narrow basement windows at the blue sky, remembering her mama's smile, laughing with her two sisters, chasing her little brother, and sitting on her father's lap. She missed her family and home so much. But there was nothing she could do. She could never earn enough money to pay the train fare to Boston, no matter how hard she worked. And when she remembered her father's hurt, angry expression when she left, she knew there was little hope of ever seeing her family again.

On Christmas Eve, the landlady of the house knocked on the basement door. Anna ran to answer, and the lady handed her a letter. Margaret knew immediately that the broadly scrawled handwriting on the envelope was her father's. With trembling fingers she pulled open the flap of the envelope. When she pulled out the single-sheet letter, two one-hundred dollar bills fell out on the floor. The letter had just three words: *"Please come home."*

Family Moment

Spend some time talking together about home and what each one loves about it. Ask, "What would you miss most about home if you had to leave?"

An Advent Prayer

Father, we are so happy to be your children and to know that we will have an eternal home in heaven with you. Home is such a beautiful word, and how can we even begin to imagine your home—its splendor, its joy, its peace and comfort and love. Help us to open our home to those who are less fortunate than we are, and to share the magnificent gifts with them that you gave to us on that first Christmas. In Jesus's name, amen.

Christmas Facts

Holly Wreaths

A popular Christmas decoration is the holly wreath—symbolic of the crown of thorns, which was pressed on the brow of Christ at the Crucifixion.

And I do come home at Christmas. We all do, or we all should. We all come home, or ought to come home, for a short holiday— the longer, the better. . . .[2]

—CHARLES DICKENS

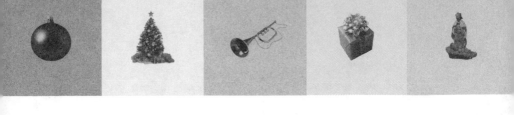

December 19

Today's Scripture:

Matthew 10:8

Heal the sick, raise the dead to life again, heal those who have skin diseases, and force demons out of people. I give you these powers freely, so help other people freely.

Suggested Longer Reading:

Acts 20:35

95

Waiting . . . Waiting for Christmas

ELIZABETH ENGLISH

Herman and I finally locked our store and dragged ourselves home to South Caldwell Street in Charlotte, North Carolina. It was 11:00 p.m., Christmas Eve of 1949. We were dog-tired.

Ours was one of those big, old general appliance stores that sold everything from refrigerators and toasters and record players to bicycles and dollhouses and games. We'd sold almost all our toys, and all the layaways, except one package, had been picked up.

Usually, Herman and I kept the store open until everything had been picked up. We knew we wouldn't have awakened very happy on Christmas morning knowing that some little child's gift was back on the layaway shelf. But the person who had put a dollar down on that package never appeared.

Early Christmas morning our twelve-year-old son, Tom, and Herman and I were out by the tree opening up gifts. But I'll tell you there was something very humdrum about this Christmas. Tom was growing up; he hadn't wanted any toys—just clothes and games. I missed his childish exuberance of past years.

As soon as breakfast was over, Tom left to visit his friend next door. And Herman disappeared into the bedroom, mumbling, "I'm going back to sleep. There's nothing left to stay up for anyway."

So there I was, alone, doing the dishes and feeling very letdown. It was nearly 9:00, and sleet mixed with snow cut the air outside. The wind rattled our windows, and I felt grateful for the warmth of the apartment. *Sure glad I don't have to go out on a day like today,* I thought to myself, picking up the wrappings and ribbons strewn around the living room.

And then it began. Something I'd never experienced before. A strange, persistent urge. "Go to the store," it seemed to say.

I looked at the icy sidewalk outside. *That's crazy,* I said to myself. I tried dismissing the thought, but it wouldn't leave me alone. *Go to the store.*

Well, I *wasn't* going to go. I'd never gone to the store on Christmas Day in the ten years we'd owned it. No one opened shop on that day. There wasn't any reason to go, and I wasn't going to.

For an hour I fought that strange feeling. Finally, I couldn't stand it any longer, and I got dressed.

"Herman," I said, feeling silly, "I think I'll walk down to the store."

Herman woke up with a start. "Whatever for? What are you going to do there?"

"Oh, I don't know," I replied lamely. "There's not much to do here. I just think I'll wander down."

He argued against it a little bit, but I told him that I'd be back soon. "Well, go on," he grumped, "but I don't see any reason for it."

I put on my gray wool coat and a gray tam on my head, then my galoshes and my red scarf and gloves. Once outside, none of these garments seemed to help. The wind cut right through me, and the sleet stung my cheeks. I groped my way along the mile down to 117 East Park Avenue, slipping and sliding all the way.

I shivered, and tucked my hands inside the pockets of my coat to keep them from freezing. I felt ridiculous. I had no business being out in that bitter chill.

There was the store just ahead. The sign announced Radio-Electronics Sales and Service, and the big glass windows jutted out onto the sidewalk. *But—What in the world?* In front of the store stood two little boys, huddled together, one about nine, and the other six.

"Here she comes!" yelled the older one. He had his arm around the younger. "See? I told you she would come!" he said jubilantly.

The two little children were half frozen. The younger one's face was wet with tears, but when he saw me, his eyes opened wide and his sobbing stopped.

"What are you two children doing out here in this freezing rain?" I scolded, hurrying them into the store and turning up the heat. "You should be at home on a day like this!" They were poorly dressed. They had no hats or gloves, and their shoes barely held together. I rubbed their small, icy hands and got them up close to the heater.

"We've been waiting for you," replied the older. They had been standing outside since 9:00, the time I normally open the store.

"Why were you waiting for me?" I asked, astonished.

"My little brother, Jimmy, didn't get any Christmas."

He touched Jimmy's shoulder. "We want to buy some skates. That's what he wants. We have these three dollars. See, Miss Lady?" he said, pulling the money from his pocket .

I looked at the dollars in his hand. I looked at their expectant faces. And then I looked around the store. "I'm sorry," I said, "but we've sold almost everything. We have no skates—" Then my eye caught sight of the layaway shelf with its one lone package. I tried to remember what was in it . . .

"Wait a minute," I told the boys. I walked over, picked up the package, unwrapped it, and, miracle of miracles, there was a pair of skates!

Jimmy reached for them. *Lord,* I said silently, *let them be his size.*

And miracle added upon miracle, they were his size.

When the older boy finished tying the laces on Jimmy's right foot and saw that the skate fit—perfectly—he stood up and presented the dollars to me.

"No, I'm not going to take your money," I told him. I *couldn't* take his money. "I want you to have these skates, and I want you to use your money to get some gloves for your hands."

The two boys just blinked at first. Then their eyes became like saucers, and their grins stretched wide when they understood I was giving them the skates, and I didn't want their three dollars.

What I saw in Jimmy's eyes was like a blessing. It was pure joy, and it was beautiful. My low spirits rose.

After the children had warmed up, I turned down the heater, and we walked out together. As I locked the door, I turned to the older brother and said, "How lucky that I happened to come along when I did. If you'd stood there much longer, you'd have frozen. But how did you boys know I would come?

I wasn't prepared for his reply. His gaze was steady, and he answered me softly, "I knew you would come," he said. "I asked Jesus to send you."

The tingles in my spine weren't from the cold. God had planned this.

As we waved goodbye, I turned home to a brighter Christmas than I had left. Tom brought his friend over to our house. Herman got out of bed, and his father, "Papa" English, and sister, Ella, came by. We had a wonderful dinner and a wonderful time.

But the one thing that made that Christmas really wonderful was the one thing that makes every Christmas wonderful: Jesus was there.[1]

Family Moment

What gifts have we been given as a family this year? Let's make a list of as many as we can.

What gifts have we given back to God and others this past year? Again, let's make a list.

Are there any adjustments that we need to make in the coming year?

An Advent Prayer

Father God, thank you that we are the recipients of so many gifts, not just this year, but each and every year. You shower down upon this family blessings that we don't even notice, yet you continue to do so. Help us this next year to be more aware of what you give to us each new day. And let us be a blessing to others by giving back to them what you have given us: love, kindness, faith, forgiveness, grace, and peace. In your name, amen.

Wise Men

The gifts that the three Wise Men, or Kings, or Magi, brought to the manger in Bethlehem cost them plenty but seem hardly appropriate to the occasion. Maybe they were all they could think of for the child who had everything. In any case, they set them down on the straw—the gold, the frankincense, the myrrh—worshiped briefly, and then returned to the East where they had come from. It gives you pause to consider how, for all their great wisdom, they overlooked the one gift that the child would have been genuinely pleased to have someday, and that was the gift of themselves and their love.[2] (See Matthew 2:1–12)

—FREDERICK BUECHNER

Christmas is coming!
Christmas . . . the season of gifts
great and small
when joy is the nicest
gift of them all.[2]

—ANONYMOUS

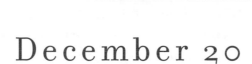

December 20

Today's Scripture:

Luke 22:19–20

Then Jesus took some bread, gave thanks, broke it, and gave it to the apostles, saying, "This is my body, which I am giving for you. Do this to remember me." In the same way, after supper, Jesus took the cup and said, "This cup is the new agreement that God makes with his people. This new agreement begins with my blood which is poured out for you."

Suggested Longer Reading:

Ephesians 2:4–10

In Remembrance of Me

WILBUR HENDRICKS

> It was December 23, 1945, and the troops were cold and lonely as their "Forty-and-Eight" boxcar rumbled through the night. The next day the train stopped at Munich, where they hoped to trade food for candles. A small ten-year-old boy nervously approached their car.

The dirty "Forty-and-Eight" was to be our home for several days as it rumbled over the railroad tracks of northern Germany. The time: December 23, 1945. We were occupation troops fresh from the States to replace battle-weary GIs, eager to return home now that the war had ended.

Our troopship had docked the day before at Bremerhaven after a rough eleven-day crossing on the cold Atlantic. Two weeks before we had mingled with happy, carefree Christmas shoppers in New York City. It was the first peacetime Christmas for our nation in four years.

Today in our "Forty-and-Eight" boxcar (a name carried over from World War I for the German boxcars that held forty men or eight mules) we were lonesome, homesick, torn apart from families and friends.

The night of December 23 was a nightmare. In the darkness we were tossed from end to end of the boxcar as it stopped and started. There were a few straw ticks provided for us if we cared to try to catch some sleep. But such attempts were useless, as those who were still standing or moving about fell over our forms on the floor in the darkness of the boxcar.

At noon on the twenty-fourth, as we sat on the floor in groups eating from the box rations that had been provided for us, one of the fellows hit upon a great idea. We passed around a transparent bag, and each of us put one item of food from our rations into the bag. We hoped that the next time the train stopped for a while we might trade the food for some candles.

One of the fellows in our group spoke German, so we asked him to negotiate for us. Our train went on and on through the German countryside. Nighttime came and still we were going. We had just about given up hope when we pulled into the large railroad yards at Munich and stopped.

Our friend immediately began calling out into the darkness. Soon a small frail boy of about ten slowly approached our car. We could imagine his fear as just a few months before we had been his country's enemy. He was baffled that one of us knew his language so well, and what did we want of him? One of the men struck a match and the bag glistened beautifully. Our spokesman explained to the boy that the bag of food would be his if he could get some candles to us before we left. His mouth gaped open, his eyes stared at the bag for a moment, then he dashed off into the darkness. We didn't realize then that there probably was more food in that bag than he had ever seen at one time.

With each creak and groan of our car we felt sure our train was leaving. But after what seemed an eternity we could see the boy's form coming back toward us, sometimes almost falling over the tracks as he ran.

One of the fellows lit a match as the boy reached the side of our car. He set a brown bag on the floor. In it were eight homemade candles in cupcake papers. We immediately lit one, and it cast a feeble but warm glow in our boxcar. We decided not to light more than one at a time in hopes that the eight might last the entire night. We thanked the boy and gave him the food. He then pulled his other hand from behind his back. In it he held a branch from a Christmas tree, about eighteen inches long. On it was a single strand of tinsel. We set it in the crack in the floor. The tinsel sparkled in the crisp breeze and reflected the glow of our flickering candle.

Then we heard sounds that told us our train was on its way. We shouted thanks to the boy as he stood and waved good-bye to us.

A deep silence fell over our group, and slowly we gathered into a circle around our candle and "tree." Some in front sat cross-legged on the floor. Others knelt behind them, and the third row stood. I don't recall just who regally began, but we took turns at our Christmas Eve worship service. We didn't have enough light to read our pocket-size New Testaments, but we recited some Scriptures the best we could from memory. We sang Christmas carols, there were sentence prayers, and one of the fellows gave a short impromptu meditation.

And then we had communion. We had no bread or wine, but we spoke the words—"Take, eat: this is my body, which is broken for you"—and we touched our lips. Then, "This cup is the new testament in my blood: this do ye, as oft as ye drink it, in remembrance of me." Again, we touched our lips. Softly we sang "Silent Night," then spoke a benediction.

Slowly the circle broke up. Our loneliness and homesickness seemed to be gone. We felt a great friendship toward one another. We knew we had just been given the greatest gift we had ever received.

Many Christmases have come and gone, and I've attended communion almost every Christmas Eve. The services have been beautiful with tall lighted tapers, silver service, plush carpeting—everything to make a beautiful experience. These services have meant a lot to me, but my thoughts still go back many years to a dirty boxcar, a circle of lonely GIs, a homemade candle in a cupcake paper, a tree branch with a lone strand of tinsel, a frail German boy, and the solemn words *"Do this in remembrance of me."*[1]

Family Moment

Why not have a private family communion "in remembrance" of Jesus and what he has done for you? Talk about the bread and wine and of what they remind us.

An Advent Prayer

Loving Father, we come now in humble gratitude and remembrance of the incredible sacrifice you made for us in allowing your Son to take our place on the cross. We are overwhelmed by your grace and love. And we praise your matchless name with our limited abilities and insufficient words. Thank you, Father, for sending your Son into the world to save us. Help us always remember what you and he have done for us, at Christmas and on every day of our lives. We love you, Lord. In Jesus's holy name we pray, amen.

The Whole World Comes to Bethlehem on Christmas Day

WILMA W. BURTON

The whole world comes to Bethlehem on Christmas Day
To walk the paths the shepherds trod
While heaven's choir sang praise to God,
Where wise men bearing gold and myrrh
Beheld the star that led them there.

The whole world comes to Bethlehem on Christmas Day
To pause before a manger's door
Where lambs bleat low upon the floor,
There to find an infant sleeping
While angels watch are sweetly keeping.

The whole world comes to Bethlehem on Christmas Day,
And though the room is humble, small,
There is a place for one and all
To enter in and worship here
The newborn Saviour they hold dear.[2]

More Meaning

Remind yourself that the holiday season can be lonely for people who are without their families, or cooped up in nursing homes, prisons, orphanages, and other similar institutions. Make every effort to expand your holiday celebration by sharing it with others who are less fortunate. Take some baked goods to a lonely older person and share several hours with him or her. Contribute some toys for children to other holiday programs for the needy, and give of your time as well. Sharing with others in less fortunate circumstances is what the holiday season is supposed to be about.[3]

— W. DYER

Then let the holly red
be hung,
And all the sweetest
carols sung,
While we with joy
remember them—
The journeys to
Bethlehem.

—FRANK DEMPSTER SHERMAN

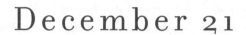

December 21

Today's Scripture:

Matthew 20:27–28

Whoever wants to become first among you must serve the rest of you like a slave. In the same way, the Son of Man did not come to be served. He came to serve others and to give his life as a ransom for many people.

Suggested Longer Reading:

Matthew 20:20–28

The Gift of the Magi

O. HENRY

One dollar and eighty-seven cents. That was all. And sixty cents of it was in pennies. Pennies saved one and two at a time by bulldozing the grocer and the vegetable man and the butcher until one's cheeks burned with the silent imputation of parsimony that such close dealing implied. Three times Della counted it. One dollar and eighty-seven cents. And the next day would be Christmas.

There was clearly nothing to do but flop down on the shabby little couch and howl. So Della did it. Which instigates the moral reflection that life is made up of sobs, sniffles, and smiles, with sniffles predominating.

While the mistress of the home is gradually subsiding from the first stage to the second, take a look at the home. A furnished flat at eight dollars per week. It did not exactly beggar description, but it certainly had that word on the lookout for the mendicancy squad.

In the vestibule below was a letterbox into which no letter would go, and an electric button from which no mortal finger could coax a ring. Also appertaining hereunto was a card bearing the name "Mr. James Dillingham Young."

The "Dillingham" had been flung to the breeze during a former period of prosperity when its possessor was being paid thirty dollars per week. Now, the income was shrunk to twenty dollars, the letters of "Dillingham" looked blurred, as though they were thinking seriously of contracting to a modest and unassuming D. But whenever Mr. James Dillingham Young came home and reached his flat above he was called "Jim" and greatly hugged by Mrs. James Dillingham Young, already introduced to you as Della. Which is all very good.

Della finished her cry and attended to her cheeks with the powder rag. She stood by the window and looked out dully at a gray cat walking a gray fence in a gray backyard. Tomorrow would be Christmas Day, and she had only one dollar and eight-seven cents with which to buy Jim a present. She had been saving every penny she could for months, with this result. Twenty dollars a week doesn't go far. Expenses had been greater than she had calculated. They always are. Only one dollar and eighty-seven cents to buy a present for Jim. Her Jim. Many a happy hour she had spent planning for something nice for him. Something fine and rare and sterling—something just a little bit near to being worthy of the honor of being owned by Jim.

There was a pier-glass between the windows of the room. Perhaps you have seen a pier-glass in an eight-dollar flat. A very thin and very agile person may, by observing his reflection in a rapid sequence of longitudinal strips, obtain a fairly accurate conception of his looks. Della, being slender, had mastered the art.

Suddenly she whirled from the window and stood before the glass. Her eyes were shining brilliantly, but her face had lost its color within twenty seconds. Rapidly she pulled down her hair and let it fall to its full length.

Now, there were two possessions of the James Dillingham Youngs in which they both took a mighty pride. One was Jim's gold watch that had been his father's and his grandfather's. The other was Della's hair. Had the Queen of Sheba lived in the flat across the airshaft, Della would have let her hair hang out the window some day to dry just to depreciate Her Majesty's jewels and gifts. Had King Solomon been the janitor, with all his treasure piled up in the basement, Jim would have pulled out his watch every time he passed, just to see him pluck at his beard from envy.

So now Della's beautiful hair fell about her rippling and shining like a cascade of brown waters. It reached below her knee and made itself almost a garment for her. And then she did it up again nervously and quickly. Once she faltered for a minute and stood still while a tear or two splashed on the worn red carpet.

On went her old brown jacket; on went her old brown hat. With a whirl of skirts and with the brilliant sparkle still in her eyes, she fluttered out the door and down the stairs to the street.

Where she stopped the sign read: "Mme. Sofronie, Hair Goods of All Kinds." One flight up Della ran, and collected herself, panting. Madame, large, too white, chilly, hardly looked the "Sofronie."

"Will you buy my hair?" asked Della. "I buy hair," said Madame. "Take yer hat off and let's have a sight looks of it." Down rippled the brown cascade. "Twenty dollars," said Madame, lifting the mass with a practiced hand. "Give it to me quick," said Della.

Oh, and the next two hours tripped by on rosy wings. Forget the hashed metaphor. She was ransacking the stores for Jim's present.

She found it at last. It surely had been made for Jim and no one else. There was no other like it in any of the stores, and she had turned all of them inside out. It was a platinum fob chain simple and chaste by meretricious ornamentation—as all good things should do. It was even worthy of The Watch. As soon as she saw it she knew that it must be Jim's. It was like him. Quietness and value—the description applied to both. Twenty-one dollars they took from her for it, and she hurried home with the 87 cents. With that chain on his watch Jim might be properly anxious about the time in any company. Grand as the watch was, he sometimes looked at it on the sly on account of the old leather strap that he used in place of a chain.

When Della reached home her intoxication gave way a little to prudence and reason. She got out her curling irons and lighted the gas and went to work repairing the ravages made by generosity added to love. Which is always a tremendous task, dear friends—a mammoth task.

Within forty minutes her head was covered with tiny, close-lying curls that made her look wonderfully like a truant schoolboy. She looked at her reflection in the mirror long, carefully, and critically.

"If Jim doesn't kill me," she said to herself, "before he takes a second look at me, he'll say I look like a Coney Island chorus girl. But what could I do—oh! What could I do with a dollar and eighty-seven cents?"

At seven 'clock the coffee was made and the frying-pan was on the back of the stove hot and ready to cook the chops.

Jim was never late. Della doubled the fob chain in her hand and sat on the corner of the table near the door that he always entered. Then she heard his step on the stairway down on the first flight, and she turned white for just a moment. She had a habit of saying little silent prayers about the simplest everyday things, and now she whispered: "Please God, make him think I am still pretty."

The door opened and Jim stepped in and closed it. He looked thin and very serious. Poor fellow, he was only twenty-two—and to be burdened with a family! He needed a new overcoat and he was without gloves.

Jim stopped inside the door, as immovable as a setter at the scent of quail. His eyes were fixed upon Della, and there was an expression in them that she could not read, and it terrified her. It was not anger, nor surprise, nor disapproval, nor horror, nor any of the sentiments that she had been prepared for. He simply stared at her fixedly with the peculiar expression on his face.

Della wriggled off the table and went for him.

"Jim, darling," she cried, "don't look at me that way. I had my hair cut off and sold it because I couldn't have lived through Christmas without giving you a present. It'll grow out again—you won't mind will you? I just had to do it. My hair grows awfully fast. Say 'Merry Christmas!' Jim and let's be happy. You don't know what a nice—what a beautiful, nice gift I've got for you."

"You've cut off your hair?" asked Jim, laboriously, as if he had not arrived at that patent fact yet even after the hardest mental labor. "Cut if off and sold it," said Della. "Don't you like me just as well anyhow? I'm me without my hair, ain't I?" Jim looked about the room curiously. "You say your hair is gone?" he said, with an air almost of idiocy.

"You needn't look for it," said Della. "It's sold, I tell you—sold and gone, too. It's Christmas Eve, boy. Be good to me, for it went for you. Maybe the hairs of my head were numbered," she went on with a sudden serious sweetness, "but nobody could ever count my love for you. Shall I put the chops on, Jim?"

Out of his trance Jim seemed quickly to wake. He enfolded his Della. For ten seconds let us regard with discreet scrutiny some inconsequential object in the other direction. Eight dollars a week or a million a year—what is the difference? A mathematician or a wit would give you the wrong answer. The magi brought valuable gifts, but that was not among them. This dark assertion will be illuminated later on.

Jim drew a package from his overcoat pocket and threw it upon the table.

"Don't make my mistake, Dell," he said, "about me. I don't think there's anything in the way of a haircut or a shave or a shampoo that could make me like my girl any less. But if you'll unwrap that package you may see why you had me going a while at first."

White fingers nimble and quick tore at the string and paper. And then an ecstatic scream of joy; and then, alas! a quick feminine change to hysterical tears and wails, necessitating the immediate employment of all the comforting powers of the lord of the flat.

For there lay The Combs—the set of combs, side and back, that Della had worshipped for so long in a Broadway window. Beautiful combs, pure tortoise shell, with jeweled rims—just the shade to wear in her beautiful vanished hair. They were expensive combs, she knew, and her heart had simply craved and yearned over them without the least hope of possession. And now, they were hers, but the tresses that should have adorned the coveted adornments were gone.

But she hugged them to her bosom, and at length she was able to look up with dim eyes and a smile and say: "My hair grows so fast, Jim!"

And then Della leaped up like a little singed cat and cried, "Oh, oh!"

Jim had not yet seen his beautiful present. She held it out to him eagerly upon her open palm. The dull precious metal seemed to flash with a reflection of her bright and ardent spirit.

"Isn't it dandy, Jim? I hunted all over town to find it. You'll have to look at the time a hundred times a day now. Give me your watch. I want to see how it looks on it."

Instead of obeying, Jim tumbled down on the couch and put his hands under the back of his head and smiled. "Dell," said he, "let's put our Christmas presents away and keep 'em a while. They're too nice to use just at present. I sold the watch to get the money to buy your combs. And now suppose you put the chops on."

The magi, as you know, were wise men—wonderfully wise men—who brought gifts to the Babe in the manger. They invented the art of giving Christmas presents. Being wise, their gifts were no doubt wise ones, possibly bearing the privilege of exchange or duplication. And here I have lamely related to you the uneventful chronicle of two foolish children in a flat who most unwisely sacrificed for each other the greatest treasures of their house.

But in a last word to the wise of these days, let it be said that of all who give gifts these two were the wisest. Of all who give and receive gifts, such as they are wisest. Everywhere they are wisest. They are the magi.[1]

Family Moment

Where were you when you first heard the message about Jesus? Did it sink in right away, or did it take some time?

When you tell the story about Jesus, what parts of the story do you talk about?

An Advent Prayer

Our Father in heaven, we're in awe that you've entrusted us with a message so wonderful. You didn't come to us with bands of angels to announce it to us, but we have heard and understood it anyway. Lord, sometimes it's a message that is hard to share with others. Give us the courage and faith to share this wonderful great news to all who will hear, so that all may know how much you love them. In the name of Jesus, amen.

Angels We Have Heard On High

Traditional French

Joyously

1. An - gels we have heard on high, Sweet - ly sing - ing o'er the plains

And the moun - tains in re - ply, Ech - o - ing their joy - ous strains.

Refrain

Glo - ri - a

in ex - cel - sis De - o *Glo -*

ri - a in ex - cel - sis De - o.

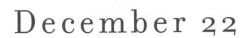

December 22

Today's Scripture:

Ecclesiastes 3:7

> There is a time to tear apart and a time to sew together.
> There is a time to be silent and a time to speak.

Suggested Longer Reading:

Ecclesiastes 3:1–11

The Story of Silent Night

CHRISTOPHER AND MELODIE LANE

Though the town of Bethlehem may have been relatively quiet when Jesus was born, it was probably not silent. Crowds of weary travelers were constantly arriving to be counted in the census. They walked the streets searching for places to stay, grumbling as they were turned away from the inn. Tired children whined, women with aching feet complained. And even in the stable where Mary and Joseph took refuge, the donkeys and cows would have continued to produce a variety of grunts and snorts.

Mohr's song speaks not of a natural silence. It captures a moment of peace, a holy hush that surely settled over Bethlehem as all of heaven viewed with wonder the birth of the God/Man. The Potter had entered into the clay that he himself had made, and he now rested in the arms of his own creation.

Because the Christmas season is so hectic and rushed, we often find it difficult to identify with the "holy hush" of that night. But Scripture implores us to make a practice of pausing from our daily routines—in all seasons—to wait upon God and to listen for his still small voice. As Frederick William Faber once explained, "Whenever the sounds of the world die out in the soul, or sink low, then we hear the whisperings of God."[1]

Family Moment

Read and pray through the following verses. Ask the Lord to draw you into the awesome silence of his presence and whisper his truth in your ear.

> "Go out and stand before me on the mountain," the Lord told him. And as Elijah stood there, the Lord passed by, and a mighty windstorm hit the mountain. It was such a terrible blast that the rocks were torn loose, but the Lord was not in the wind. After the wind there was an earthquake, but the Lord was not in the earthquake. And after the earthquake there was a fire, but the Lord was not in

the fire. And after the fire there was the sound of a gentle whisper. (1 Kings 19:11–12, NLT)

The Lord is wonderfully good to those who wait for him and seek him. So it is good to wait quietly for salvation from the Lord. (Lamentations 3:25–26, NLT)

Be silent, and know that I am God! I will be honored by every nation. I will be honored throughout the world. (Psalm 46:10, NLT)

An Advent Prayer

Lord, I invite your Spirit to come upon me and calm my busy mind. Quiet my heart as I wait before you. In the silence let me hear you. In the stillness let me know you. Open my eyes that I may see your glory and receive the grace you have extended to me today. In Jesus's name, amen.

"Stille Nacht"

Many interesting fables abound for the origins of "Silent Night." Most of them are fanciful and untrue.

The Christmas Eve of 1818 was at hand. Pastor Joseph Mohr of St. Nicholas Church in Oberndorf, Austria, decided that he needed a carol for the Christmas Eve service. The little poem he had written two years earlier while serving at the pilgrim church in Mariapfarr just might work. Perhaps this poem could be set to music. He hurried off to see his friend, Franz Xaver Gruber, who was a schoolteacher and also served as the church's organist and choir master. Maybe he could help. He did.

In a few short hours Franz came up with the hauntingly beautiful melody that is so loved and revered to this day. At the request of Joseph, who had a special love for his guitar, Franz composed the music for guitar accompaniment. Just a few short hours later, Franz stood with his friend the pastor, Joseph, in front of the altar in St. Nicholas church and introduced "Stille Nacht" to the congregation.

Silent Night

Joseph Mohr

Franz Gruber

1. Si - lent night, Ho - ly night, All is calm, All is bright, Round yon vir — gin Moth-er and child. Ho - ly In - fant so ten - der and mild, Sleep in heav - en - ly peace, ___ Sleep — in heav - en - ly peace!

2.
Silent night, holy night,
Shepherds quake at the sight;
Glories stream from heaven afar,
Heavenly hosts sing *alleluia,*
Christ, the Savior is born!
Christ, the Savior is born!

3.
Silent night, holy night,
Son of God, love's pure light
Radiant beams from Thy holy face,
With the dawn of redeeming grace,
Jesus Lord, at Thy Birth,
Jesus Lord, at Thy Birth.

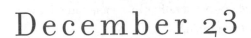

December 23

Today's Scripture:

Luke 1:46–48

Then Mary said, "My soul praises the Lord; my heart rejoices in God my Savior, because he has shown his concern for his humble servant girl. From now on, all people will say that I am blessed."

Suggested Longer Reading:

Luke 1:39–56

A Gathering of Angels

CALVIN MILLER

Christmas Eve had come at last. Gabriel and Michael sat talking.

"What time is it, Gabriel?" asked Michael.

Gabriel looked down at a rather immense calendar watch, studied it a moment, and looked back up.

"It's exactly the fourteenth year of Augustus . . . you know, annus quattuordecimus, as these Romans say."

"No, no, no! I want it in the new time. I can't remember! Is it BC or AD?"

Gabriel looked again at the big watch.

"It's about time for the changeover! Tonight at midnight, the Lord God puts the new star on that elliptical orbit that passes over Bethlehem . . . then all the angels have to set their watches ahead to AD."

Michael scratched his head.

"AD? What's that mean?"

"How do I know what it means? The Lord God's the only one who knows everything. I think it stands for some more of those Roman words, *anno domini* or something like that. Anyway, it just means Jesus Time. The whole world is going to use it; it all becomes official as soon as the Lord God takes the brakes off that new star."

Michael cautiously ventured one final question.

"Look, Gabriel, how are they coming on that new star?"

Gabriel looked excited.

"I just flew by the Star Foundry yesterday. Mike, this is going to be a big one. Bright too. You remember how all the angels were wearing sunglasses when the Lord God started dumping the hydrogen in Andromeda? Well, I swear! This one's bigger and brighter. It makes Halley's comet look like a sulfur match."

"Sulfur match?"

"Never mind, Michael. They're pumping the helium in now. This is going to be some star. It's gonna slam smack into the middle of the constellation Pisces. They're some astrologers out in the desert at a big stargazers convention. Those guys are really in for a surprise. Remember how mixed up they were during the last meteorite shower? Think what it'll do to their charts when Redeemer I comes a-slicin' through the sky."

Michael beamed. "Redeemer I . . . I like that. Is that what they're calling it: Redeemer I?"

"That's what it is, Michael."

"Man, what a name for the Jesus star! Say, speaking of Jesus, where is he, Gabe?"

"Still tucked up under the heart of Mary, but not for long. Mike, I'm so excited!"

"Me too. I've been practicing the Christmas music all day long. I hate scaring those shepherds like we're going to have to do. Still, I know I can't hold my song past midnight."

"Me either, Gabe. I understand the whole anthem is going to be in Aramaic. Of course, I really sing it best in Latin—you know, like *Gloria in excelsis Deo.* But you know the Lord God. Those shepherds don't know a word of Latin, so we're going to do the whole thing in Aramaic."

Michael paused and walked a few steps and looked over the crystal balustrades.

"Look, Gabriel. See the little couple down there? They've been traveling for three days."

Gabriel leaned out and looked over. He struggled to fight back tears before he spoke. "He's been to all six inns in the city. She's in so much pain she can hardly stand it. She's only eighteen and this is her first baby."

"Look! Gabriel, they're going toward the stable. It must be getting time."

"Say, what the . . . what's that light?"

"Wow, Gabe, look. It's Redeemer I. Better get into your choir robe."
Quickly Gabriel slipped into his choir robe.

Redeemer I rolled out into the night sky and spilled its light.

Everything was all golden!

It was magnificent!

Down below, the astrologers panicked in the splendor of the light.
Nervously Gabriel continued to play with the stem of his watch. Ten thousand

angels stood in rapt attention waiting for the downbeat of the Aramaic anthem.

Far to the left of Damascus, the shepherds gazed out into the night silently. The universe was hushed. Nothing moved.

Then the great Lord God of all the universe raised his hands. The great Redeemer I rolled right over Bethlehem. The prophet Micah beamed from ear to ear. And the Lord God dropped his hand.

And distinctly every angel heard a faint redeeming sound above the sleeping world. At that very moment when God dropped his hand, they heard it. A baby cried!

And Gabriel set his watch to run a billion years on Jesus Time.[1]

Family Moment

It's the day before Christmas Eve. Ask family members what they are looking forward to the most as the celebration is ready to begin.

Is there anything this family has missed as we've prepared our hearts for Christmas?

An Advent Prayer

We pray to you, O Lord Jesus: You were born once, once for all, so that you also would die once, but once for all. These two moments do not need to repeat themselves in your life—only in ours as faith recalls the moments and celebrates them again.

But this is our prayer for the coming Christmas: O Lord Jesus, be your own messenger unto us. By your graceful presence in our hearts, in the bosoms of our families, in the gatherings that will worship to rejoice in your nativity again, be there the source of light and life and rebirth—not so much your own as our own. O Lord Jesus, be born in us today, that we might rise up, filled with your light, knowing your joy, strong in your walking, filled with your purpose and bright unto the world itself. We pray this even now as we hold our breath against that eve in which you were born. Amen.[2]

—WALTER WANGERIN JR.

December 24

Today's Scripture:

Luke 2:13–14

Then a very large group of angels from heaven joined the first angel, praising God and saying: "Give glory to God in heaven, and on earth let there be peace among the people who please God."

Suggested Longer Reading:

Luke 2:8–14

Christmas Night

Max Lucado

It's Christmas night. The house is quiet. Even the crackle is gone from the fireplace. Warm coals issue a lighthouse glow in the darkened den. Stockings hang empty on the mantle. The tree stands naked in the corner. Christmas cards, tinsel, and memories remind Christmas night of Christmas Day.

It's Christmas night. What a day it has been! Spiced tea. Santa Claus. Cranberry sauce. "Thank you so much." "You shouldn't have!" "Grandma is on the phone." Knee-deep wrapping paper. "It just fits." Flashing cameras.

It's Christmas night. The tree that only yesterday grew from soil made of gifts, again grows from the Christmas tree stand. Presents are now possessions. Wrapping paper is bagged and in the dumpster. The dishes are washed and leftover turkey awaits next week's sandwiches.

It's Christmas night. The last of the carolers appeared on the ten o'clock news. The last of the apple pie was eaten by my brother-in-law. And the last of the Christmas albums have been stored away having dutifully performed their annual rendition of chestnuts, white Christmases, and red-nosed reindeer.

It's Christmas night.

The midnight hour has chimed and I should be asleep, but I'm awake. I'm kept awake by one stunning thought. The world was different this week. It was temporarily transformed.

The magical dust of Christmas glittered on the cheeks of humanity ever so briefly, reminding us of what is worth having and what we were intended to be. We forgot our compulsion with winning, wooing, and warring. We put away our ladders and ledgers, we hung up our stopwatches and weapons. We stepped off our racetracks and roller coasters and looked outward toward the star of Bethlehem.

It's the season to be jolly because, more than at any other time, we think of Him. More than in any other season, His name is on our lips.

And the results? For a few precious hours our heavenly yearnings intermesh and we become a chorus. A ragtag chorus of longshoremen, Boston lawyers, illegal immigrants, housewives, and a thousand other peculiar persons who are banking that Bethlehem's mystery is in reality, a reality. "Come and behold Him" we sing, stirring even the sleepiest of shepherds and pointing them toward the Christ-child.

For a few precious hours, He is beheld. Christ the Lord. Those who pass the year without seeing Him, suddenly see Him. People who have been accustomed to using His name in vain, pause to use it in praise. Eyes, now free of the blinders of self, marvel at His majesty.

All of a sudden He's everywhere.

In the grin of the policeman as he drives the paddy wagon full of presents to the orphanage.

In the twinkle in the eyes of the Taiwanese waiter as he tells of his upcoming Christmas trip to see his children.

In the emotion of the father who is too thankful to finish the dinner table prayer.

He's in the tear of the mother as she welcomes home her son from overseas.

He's in the heart of the man who spent Christmas morning on skid row giving away cold baloney sandwiches and warm wishes.

He's in the solemn silence of the crowd of shopping mall shoppers as the elementary school chorus sings "Away in a Manger."

Emmanuel. He is with us. God came near.

It's Christmas night. In a few hours the cleanup will begin—lights will come down, trees will be thrown out. Size thirty-six will be exchanged for size forty, eggnog will be on sale for half price. Soon life will be normal again. December's generosity will become January's payments, and the magic will begin to fade.

But for the moment, the magic is still in the air. Maybe that's why I'm still awake. I want to savor the spirit just a bit more. I want to pray that those who beheld Him today will look for Him next August. And I can't help but linger on one fanciful thought: if He can do so much with such timid prayers offered in December, how much more could He do if we thought of Him every day?[1]

Family Moment

Once in a while, some small portion of writing comes along that no one seems to know from where it came, but it has an impact that is both deep and wide. The simple letter below is one such piece of writing. Have someone read it, then discuss what it means to each family member.

Letter from Jesus

Dear Friend:

How are you? I just had to send you this letter to tell you how much I love and care about you. I saw you yesterday as you were walking with friends. I waited all day hoping you would talk to me also. As evening drew near, I gave you a sunset to close your day, a cool breeze to rest you, and I waited. You never came. Oh, yes, it hurt me, but I still love you, because I am your friend.

I saw you fall asleep last night, and I longed to touch your brow, so I spilled moonlight upon your pillow and face. Again I waited, wanting to rush down so we could talk. I have so many gifts for you.

You awakened late and rushed off for the day—my tears were in the rain. Today you looked so sad, so alone. It makes my heart ache because I understand. My friends let me down and hurt me many times, too, but I love you. I try to tell you in the quiet green grass. I whisper it in the leaves and the trees, and give it in the color of the flowers. I shout it to you in the mountain streams, and give the birds love songs to sing. I clothe you with warm sunshine and perfume the air. My love for you is deeper than the oceans, and bigger than the biggest want or need you have.

We will spend eternity together in heaven. I know how hard it is on this earth, I really know . . . My father wants to help you too . . . He's that way, you know. Just call on me, ask me, talk to me . . . But if you don't call, you'll see . . . I have chosen you and because of this, I will wait . . . because I love you.

Your friend Jesus

An Advent Prayer

Lord Jesus, you are our friend. You think about us more times each day than we could ever count. I'm sorry . . . we're sorry, that we don't give you our attention throughout the day even more. But we also know that you're not discouraged about this. We know that you wait for us, and are glad whenever our hearts turn your direction. Help us to do that even more in the coming year ahead. Amen.

December 25

Today's Scripture:

John 8:31

So Jesus said to the Jews who believed in him, "If you continue to obey my teaching, you are truly my followers."

Suggested Longer Reading:

John 3:31–36

Ragman

WALTER WANGERIN

> *Walter Wangerin is one of the most profound religious thinkers and artists of our
> time. In this wholly fictional talk, he shows how Christ meets everyone's special
> needs in a very special way. The uniqueness of the Christian experience is that
> Jesus is just what he needs to be to meet anyone's particular need.*

I saw a strange sight, I stumbled upon a story most strange, like nothing my life, my street sense, my sly tongue had ever prepared me for.

Hush, child. Hush, now, and I will tell it to you.

Even before the dawn one Friday morning I noticed a young man, handsome and strong, walking the alleys of our city. He was pulling an old cart filled with clothes both bright and new, and he was calling in a clear, tenor voice: "Rags!" Ah, the air was foul and the first light filthy to be crossed by such sweet music.

"Rags! New rags for old! I take your tired rags! Rags!"

"Now, this is a wonder," I thought to myself, for the man stood six-feet-four, and his arms were like tree limbs, hard and muscular, and his eyes flashed intelligence. Could he find no better job than this, to be a ragman in the inner city?

I followed him. My curiosity drove me. And I wasn't disappointed.

Soon the Ragman saw a woman sitting on her back porch. She was sobbing into a handkerchief, sighing, and shedding a thousand tears. Her knees and elbows made a sad X. Her shoulders shook. Her heart was breaking.

The Ragman stopped his cart. Quietly, he walked to the woman, stepping round tin cans, dead toys, and Pampers.

"Give me your rag," he said so gently, "and I'll give you another."

He slipped the handkerchief from her eyes. She looked up, and he laid across her palm a linen cloth so clean and new that it shined. She blinked from the gift to the giver.

Then, as he began to pull his cart again, the Ragman did a strange thing: he put her stained handkerchief to his own face; and then he began to weep, to sob as grievously as she had done, his shoulders shaking. Yet she was left without a tear.

"This is a wonder," I breathed to myself, and I followed the sobbing Ragman like a child who cannot turn away from mystery.

"Rags! Rags! New rags for old!"

In a little while, when the sky showed gray behind the rooftops and I could see the shredded curtains hanging out black windows, the Ragman came upon a girl whose head was wrapped in a bandage, whose eyes were empty. Blood soaked her bandage. A single line of blood ran down her cheek.

How the tall Ragman looked upon this child with pity, and he drew a lovely yellow bonnet from his cart.

"Give me your rag," he said, tracing his own line on her cheek, "and I'll give you mine."

The child could only gaze at him while he loosened the bandage, removed it, and tied it to his own head. The bonnet he set on hers. And I gasped at what I saw: for with the bandage went the wound! Against his brow it ran a darker, more substantial blood—his own!

"Rags! Rags! I take old rags!" cried the sobbing, bleeding, strong, intelligent Ragman.

The sun hurt both the sky, now, and my eyes; the Ragman seemed more and more to hurry.

"Are you going to work?" he asked a man who leaned against a telephone pole. The man shook his head.

The Ragman pressed him. "Do you have a job?"

"Are you crazy?" sneered the other. He pulled away from the pole, revealing the right sleeve of his jacket—flat, the cuff stuffed into the pocket. He had no arm.

"So," said the Ragman, "give me your jacket, and I'll give you mine."

Such quiet authority in his voice!

The one-armed man took off his jacket. So did the Ragman—and I trembled at what I saw: for the Ragman's arm stayed in its sleeve, and when the other put it on he had two good arms, thick as tree limbs, but the Ragman had only one.

"Go to work," he said.

After that he found a drunk, lying unconscious beneath an army blanket, an old man, hunched, wizened, and sick. He took that blanket and wrapped it round himself, but for the drunk he left new clothes.

And now I had to run to keep up with the Ragman. Though he was weeping uncontrollably, and bleeding freely at the forehead, pulling his cart with one arm, stumbling for drunkenness, falling again and again, exhausted, old, and sick, yet he went with terrible speed. On spider's legs he skittered through the alleys of the city, this mile and the next, until he came to its limits, and then he rushed beyond.

I wept to see the change in this man. I hurt to see his sorrow. And yet I needed to see where he was going in such haste, perhaps to know what drove him so.

The little old Ragman—he came to a landfill. He came to the garbage pits. And then I wanted to help him in what he did, but I hung back, hiding. He climbed a hill. With tormented labor he cleared a little space on that hill. Then he sighed. He lay down. He pillowed his head on a handkerchief and a jacket. He covered his bones with an army blanket. And he died.

Oh, how I cried to witness that death! I slumped in a junked car and wailed and mourned as one who has no hope because I had come to love the Ragman. Every other face had faded in the wonder of this man, and I cherished him, but he died. I sobbed myself to sleep.

I did not know—how could I know?—that I slept through Friday night and Saturday and its night, too.

But then, on Sunday morning, I was wakened by a violence.

Light—pure, hard, demanding light—slammed against my sour face, and I blinked, and I looked, and I saw the last and the first wonder of all. There was the Ragman, folding the blanket most carefully, a scar on his forehead, but alive! And, besides that, healthy! There was no sign of sorrow nor of age, and all the rags that he had gathered shined for cleanliness.

Well, then I lowered my head and, trembling for all that I had seen, I myself walked up to the Ragman. I told him my name with shame, for I was a sorry figure next to him. Then I took off all my clothes in that place, and I said to him with dear yearning in my voice: "Dress me."

He dressed me. My Lord, he put new rags on me, and I am a wonder beside him. The Ragman, the Ragman, the Christ![1]

Family Moment

What do you think this story means? How should we respond to the story?

An Advent Prayer

Dear Father in heaven, the message of Advent and Christmas points directly to the message of Easter. We thank you for invading our world, our hearts, and trading our rags for your riches. You have done a beautiful thing for us, a gift so great that we can never repay you. But you didn't ask us to repay it, you asked us to accept it. So today, the day we celebrate your birth, we accept your gift to us with a heart that longs to know you better. Help us to be satisfied with the knowledge that you are in our hearts, but help us not to be satisfied with our knowledge of you and your love for us. Show us each new day how much you love, how much you care, and how much you want to open up the windows of heaven . . . for us. In your strong name, Lord Jesus, we say to you, "Happy birthday!"

In the Bleak Mid-Winter

What can I give Him,
Poor as I am?
If I were a shepherd,
I would bring a lamb,
If I were a Wise Man,
I would do my part,
Yet what can I give Him?
Give my heart.

—CHRISTINA ROSSETTI

Christ uncrowned himself to crown us,
and put off his robes to put on our rags,
and came down from heaven
to keep us out of hell.
He fasted forty days that he might
feast us for all eternity;
he came from heaven to earth
that he might send us
from earth to heaven.[2]

—W. Dyer

NOTES

Reasonable efforts have been made to locate the primary copyright holders of all the material in this book. However, some authors and original sources are still unknown. If anyone can provide knowledge of the authorship, origin, and first publication source for these stories, please relay this information to Greg Johnson c/o Editorial Department, W Publishing Group, P. O. Box 141000, Nashville, TN 37217.

Prologue

1. Charles Dickens, "The Life of My Lord for My Dear Children" from *The Book of Jesus*, Calvin Miller (New York, NY: Simon & Schuster, 1996), 130–133.

Day 1

1. Angela Elwell Hunt, "Avner and the Morning Star," ©1994. Reprinted by permission of the author.
2. Joe L. Wheeler, "The 36 Days of Christmas," Copyright ©1997. Reprinted by permission of the author.

Day 2

1. Gillette Jones, "The Christmas Room," © The Christian Herald Association. Reprinted with permission.
2. Wayne Dyer, *Happy Holidays* (New York, NY: HarperCollins Publishers Inc., 1986), 24. Reprinted by permission of HarperCollins Publishers Inc.

Day 3

1. Author unknown, "The Parable of the Shopper."

Day 4

1. "In Another Stable" by David Niven. Reprinted with permission from *Guideposts*. Copyright " 1963 by Guideposts, Carmel, New York 10512. All rights reserved.

Day 5

1. Gary B. Swanson, "To See Again," ©1984. Reprinted by permission of the author.
2. Wayne Dyer, *Happy Holidays* (New York, NY: William Morrow & Co., 1986), 23.

Day 6

1. Lou Cassels, "Now I Understand, Now I See Why," UPI/RSICopyright.
2. Wayne Dyer from *The Book of Jesus*, Calvin Miller (New York, NY: Simon & Schuster, 1996), 55.

Day 8

1. "A Boy's Finest Memory" by Cecille B. DeMille reprinted with permission from Guideposts. Copyright © 1947 by Guideposts, Carmel, New York 10512. All rights reserved.

2. Wayne Dyer, *Happy Holidays* (New York, NY: William Morrow & Co., 1986), 24.

Day 9

1. "Trouble at the Inn" by Dina Donahue. Reprinted with permission from *Guideposts*. Copyright © 1966 by Guideposts, Carmel, New York 10512. All rights reserved.
2. Max Lucado, *God Came Near* (Nashville, TN: W Publishing Group, 1986), 23. All rights reserved.
3. James Wallingford from *A Treasury of Christmas Joy* edited by Paul M. Miller (Colorado Springs, CO: Honor Books, a division of David C. Cook Publishers, 1999), 179.
4. *No Room* by Kathryn Slasor ©1970. Used by permission.

Day 10

1. Gene Edwards, "The Magi's Visit" from *The Birth* (Jacksonville, FL: Seed Sowers Publishing House, 1990). Used with permission.
2. Jim Bishop, *The Day Christ was Born* (New York, NY: Harper Collins, 1960). Reprinted by permission of HarperCollins Publishers Inc.

Day 11

1. Jim Bishop, *The Day Christ was Born* (New York, NY: Harper Collins, 1960). Reprinted by permission of HarperCollins Publishers Inc.

Day 12

1. Hans Christian Andersen, "The Little Match-Girl." Written in 1846. Public Domain.

Day 13

1. Heywood Broun, "A Shepherd" from *Collected Edition of Heywood Broun*. Copyright ©1941 by Heywood Hale Broun.

Day 14

1. "The Unexpected Christmas" by Marguerite Nixon. Reprinted with permission from *Guideposts*. Copyright " 1965 by Guideposts, Carmel, New York 10512. All rights reserved.
2. Charles Dickens, *A Treasury of Christmas Joy* edited by Paul M. Miller (Colorado Springs, CO: Honor Books, a division of David C. Cook Publishers, 1999), 108.

Day 15

1. Hans Christian Andersen, "The Fir Tree" from *A Treasury of Christmas Joy* edited by Paul M. Miller (Colorado Springs, CO: Honor Books, a division of David C. Cook Publishers, 1999), 99–101.

Day 16

1. "My Most Memorable Christmas" by Catherine Marshall. Reprinted with permission from *Guideposts*. Copyright © 1965 by Guideposts, Carmel, New York 10512. All rights reserved. Adapted from *Family Weekly*.

Day 17

1. "A String of Blue Beads", from *A String of Blue Beads* by Fulton Oursler, copyright 1951 by Reader's Digest Association, Inc. Used by permission of Doubleday, a division of Random House, Inc.
2. Ethel Dietrich, ©1985. Reprinted with permission from the author.

Day 19

1. "Waiting . . . Waiting for Christmas" by Elizabeth English. Reprinted with permission from *Guideposts*. Copyright © 1983 by Guideposts, Carmel, New York 10512. All rights reserved.
2. From *Peculiar Treasures: A Biblical Who's Who* by Frederick Buechner. Copyright © 1979 by Frederick Buechner. Illustration copyright © 1979 by Katherine A. Buechner. Reprinted by permission of HarperCollins Publishers Inc.

Day 20

1. Wilbur Hendricks, "In Remembrance of Me" ©1970.
2. Wilma W. Burton, "The Whole World Comes to Bethlehem on Christmas Day," quoted from *An American Christmas* (Nashville, TN: Ideals Publications, 1996), 62-63.
3. Wayne Dyer from *The Book of Jesus*, Calvin Miller (New York, NY: Simon & Schuster, 1996), 41.

Day 21

1. O. Henry, "The Gift of the Magi." Public domain.

Day 22

1. Christopher and Melodie Lane, "The Story of Silent Night" from *Christ in the Carols* (Wheaton, IL: Tyndale House Publishers, 1999), 1–3.

Day 23

1. Calvin Miller, "A Gathering of Angels," ©1975. Reprinted by permission of the author.
2. Walter Wangerin Jr., "Advent Prayer," ©1996. Printed by permission of Walker Wangerin, Jr.

Day 24

1. Max Lucado, *God Came Near* (Nashville, TN: W Publishing Group, 1986), 45–47. All rights reserved.

Day 25

1. Walter Wangerin Jr., *Ragman and Other Cries of Faith* (San Francisco, CA: HarperCollins, 1984), 3–6. Reprinted by permission of HarperCollins Publishers Inc.